THE
LITTLE
BOOK
OF
FERMANAGH

DOREEN MCBRIDE

The
History
Press
Ireland

This book is dedicated to a very dear friend, Kate Muldoon,
who was an inspiration to all who knew her.

First published 2018

The History Press Ireland
50 City Quay
Dublin 2
Ireland
www.thehistorypress.ie

© Doreen McBride, 2018

British Library Cataloguing in Publication Data.
A catalogue record for this book is available from the British Library.

ISBN 978 1 84588 981 4

Typesetting and origination by The History Press
Printed by T.J International

CONTENTS

ACKNOWLEDGEMENTS

Thanks are due to my husband George, who, when I go on field trips, continues to do his best to keep me out of trouble and who often uncovers useful information. Thanks are also due to my cousin, Vernon Finlay, for constructive criticism on the manuscript and to my dear friend Kate Muldoon, who died in December, who always provided a listening ear and encouragement. Thank you Florence Creighton, who gave me information about smuggling and the lace industry, John Reihill for providing information about island living, and Vicky Herbert, for information about Lisnaskea Workhouse, nicknames and vocabulary used in Fermanagh and who read the manuscript to ensure it reflected a Fermanagh perspective. I wish to acknowledge Fergus Cleary, chief designer of Belleek, for information about the pottery, Seamas McCanny, author and broadcaster, for quirky information and with whom I had great craic. Enniskillen Museum, Lisnaskea Library, and the Enniskillen Library staff were extremely helpful. Thanks are due to Ken McElroy, Margaret Gallagher, Pat Mahon and John McCollum for information. Fred Ternan from Lough Erne Heritage provided information about cots, and the late Angela Dillon, past President of Banbridge Historical Society told me about her grandmother's recollections of being an inmate of a fever hospital. Maíréad O'Dolan provided information about the holy well at Belcoo. I spent a fascinating morning with Alan Heuton, the Head Gardener at Castle Coole, and Heather Hamilton, Education Officer, Florencecourt, Richard Watson and John Martin McGovern from the Geopark could not have been more helpful. The illustrations are my own and the cut-outs are by Tineke Kroes.

INTRODUCTION

Fermanagh gets its name from the Fir Manach. Fir means men, so Fir Manach translates as Manach's men. They were a small tribe from County Leinster, who settled along the River Erne during the second century.

County Fermanagh is known as 'Ulster's Lakeland'. It is a land of contrasts, containing some of the best-designed modern buildings in Europe such as the award-winning South West Acute Hospital in Enniskillen, as well as some of the most ancient. There are standing stones and holy wells, remnants of pagan and Christian religions and monastic sites, such as the one on Devonish Island founded during the sixth century.

The county is a land of lakes surrounded by hills. A beautiful, peaceful place, inhabited by friendly, humorous people. It was one of the two of Ulster's nine counties that were planted by James I when he inherited the British throne from Elizabeth I in 1601 and it has been affected by the recent troubles.

Most of the early planters intermarried with the local population, which explains why many well-known Nationalists have Ulster/ Scots surnames. The majority population is Catholic, in common with four of the six counties in Ulster that make up the part of Ireland that has chosen to remain within the United Kingdom of Great Britain and Northern Ireland. Recent troubles have resulted in a fall in the number of Protestants living in Fermanagh, although they are increasing again thanks to the peace process.

In spite of its sad history a recent survey showed that Fermanagh's inhabitants are the happiest in Europe, if not the world. It has emerged from its troubled past a beautiful peaceful place, full of interest with prehistoric remains, Irish mythology, good craic, music, theatre, food, crafts and what has been described as the best boating and fishing in Europe.

1

FASCINATING FACTS ABOUT FERMANAGH

Local historian Seamus McCanny says Van Morrison wrote 'Brown Eyed Girl' on a piano in Derrygonnelly. A recording of it was released while he was 22 and his solo career was still in its infancy. The original title was 'Brown Skinned Girl', but Morrison said he made a mistake and changed the name when he'd finished recording in June 1967. It became his first American top ten single and has become a standard that gets frequent airplay, although Morrison is on record as saying, 'I've got about 300 songs I think are better.' It was listed at 109 on the *Rolling Stone* magazine list of 500 Greatest Songs of All Time in November 2004, and was inducted into the Grammy Hall of Fame in 2007.

I visited Derrygonnelly to see if I could find out more about the 'Brown Eyed Girl'. I started by visiting the Leginn Cornmill and Miller's Cottage; it's a quaint place but nobody could give me any information. I began questioning people in the main street and drew blanks until a man with an English accent said: 'I think you'll find it was written in a bar.' The main street in Derrygonnelly has several, with the Old Pal's Bar a likely-looking place to start. It is full of character, not gentrified or updated, and it had a helpful barman, Stephen Donaldson.

When asked if Van Morrison had written 'Brown Eyed Girl' in Derrygonnelly, Stephen replied:

> Yes, of course he did. I can't remember the exact year. Early in his solo career Van spent several summer months living here. He stayed, with his friend, Gerald Flanagan, in an old unoccupied house near Derrygonnelly on the lower slopes of Knockmore Mountain.

Yon brown-eyed girl was dead on!

Van was very friendly with a local girl. She was a real beauty, so she was! He sorted out his song on our piano. There's a framed photo of him on the wall in at the back. He said Gerald Flanaghan was his agent.

After showing the photograph, Stephen added: 'I believe that photo was taken by Gerald Flanagan and used on the dust cover of the original recording of "Brown Eyed Girl".'

According to Stephen, shortly afterwards Van and Gerald went to America and struck up a deal with a record company.

The rest is history. 'Brown Eyed Girl' topped the American hit parade. Unfortunately, Van and Gerald had some kind of serious disagreement and are no longer friends. As for the identity of the brown eyed girl? Natives of Derrygonnelly suspect they know who she is! She's still alive and well and living there!

❈ ❈ ❈

Local tradition states that the blind harper, Turlough O'Carolan (1688–1738), composed America's national anthem, the 'Star Spangled Banner'.

O'Carolan was born near Nobber in County Meath. He was the son of a local farmer and blacksmith who went to work with the MacDermott Roe family. Mrs MacDermott befriended the young lad and gave him an education. When he was 18 years old he contracted smallpox, which destroyed his sight so he couldn't earn a living by farming. He had a gift for writing poetry and for music, so it was decided the best thing he could do was earn a living by using his talents.

MacDermott Roe taught him to play a harp. Mrs MacDermott then gave him a horse, a harp and some money and he began a career as an itinerant musician. He quickly became well known and travelled the length and breadth of Ireland. He entertained guests in the 'big houses' because music was a way for the Anglo–Irish to keep connected with the Gaelic world after 'the flight of the earls' in 1607.

O'Carolan loved Fermanagh and spent many happy days there. It was there, while visiting Tempo Manor, he met Mary Maguire. The couple fell in love, married and produced six daughters and one son. O'Carolan was heartbroken when Mary died in 1733. He died in 1738.

O'Carolan was a gifted composer as well as a superb harper. He wrote variations on many old tunes, including Scottish songs such as 'Cock up your Beaver' and 'When She Cam Ben' as well as composing new tunes, such as 'Planxty Maguire', written for Cuchonnacht Maguire, the son of Brian Maguire who swore allegiance to James I of England after the 'flight of the earls' and was granted 2,000 acres of land around Tempo.

⚝ ⚝ ⚝

Australian author Andrew Barton 'Banjo' Patterson wrote the most recognisable of Australian songs, 'Waltzing Matilda'. He was the great-grandson of General Barton from Pettigo.

⚝ ⚝ ⚝

Roslea Hero won the All-Ireland Donkey Derby three times. This achievement is remarkable because donkeys have a reputation for being stubborn and unpredictable. That fact is emphasised by a story a young girl once told me about entering a donkey derby. She was very excited; she loved horses and wanted to become a famous jockey so she entered her pet donkey into an old nags' race to get experience. She and her donkey were doing well until disaster struck. She recalled:

> A short distance from the finishing line a dirty auld nag caught up with my poor donkey and a big thing flew past my ear. The auld nag mounted my donkey, who stopped and lost the race while the crowd laughed and cheered. I didn't know what to do. The organisers came and helped me down. They gave me a consolation prize, but I couldn't keep from crying. My daddy said I should cheer up and learn to take the rough with the smooth. Bad things happen in any career so I should just get on with it, but I don't think I want to be a jockey any more.

⚝ ⚝ ⚝

Meredith Frank Maguire, a Member of Parliament, changed the course of British history when his casting vote led to Margaret Thatcher coming to power in 1979.

Frank was an Irish Republican and an Independent Member of the British Parliament at Westminster. Born into a Republican family, he was interned during his youth for Irish Republican activities. In later life he opposed violence but remained close to the Republican movement. He ran a public house, called Frank's Bar, in Lisnaskea and in October 1974 he was elected, as a unity candidate, to represent Fermanagh and Tyrone.

Sinn Fein Members of Parliament do not recognise the British Parliament and refuse to take up seats in Westminster. Frank was an independent and took up his seat but his attendances were infrequent. He never made a full speech but he did cast some crucial votes supporting the Labour government during the 1970s. However, he is famous for 'abstaining in person', which brought the Labour government of James Callaghan down. The government lost by a single vote (311 votes to 310). This forced a general election, which was won by Margaret Thatcher's Conservative Party.

⸎ ⸎ ⸎

Paddy Monaghan from Ederney, Fermanagh, befriended Muhammad Ali and became known as Paddy-Ali.

At the time Paddy lived in Saxton Road, (one of the worst streets) in Abingdon, near Oxford in England. Paddy was a bare-knuckle boxing champion. He thought the American Government's action of stripping Ali of his world heavyweight boxing title in 1967 because he refused to fight in the Vietnam War was outrageous. He coined the phrase 'people's champion' to describe Ali, organised a petition that eventually contained 22,024 signatures and wrote to President Nixon to object.

Ali was so grateful he visited Paddy at his home in Abingdon, which was a tiny terraced house. He caused a sensation; the police couldn't hold the crowds back and the army had to be called in.

Ali entertained local children by doing magic tricks. He signed autographs, sparred with local boys, including Paddy-Ali's 16-year-old son, and had tea with the Monaghans. The two men struck up a close friendship during which Ali suggested Paddy-Ali move to the US, but Paddy-Ali declined because of family ties. He eventually left England and moved back to Ireland.

⸎ ⸎ ⸎

Folklore says Noah had a grandson called Beith. After the great flood Beith landed on Carnmore Point in County Fermanagh in an ark filled with the world's most beautiful women. Local tradition says the women fell in love with local men, resulting in the legendary beauty of Irish women.

❊ ❊ ❊

Neil Armstrong (5 August 1930–12 August 2012), the first man to step on the moon, had ancestors who came from County Fermanagh. Robert Armstrong, from Lisnaskea, was Neil Armstrong's

Good luck Mr Jones!

grandfather's brother. Neil Armstrong also had ancestors from Irvinestown. The Armstrongs were among the border reivers evicted from Scotland and planted in County Fermanagh during the early seventeenth century. (Reivers caused mayhem by conducting raids along the border between England and Scotland.)

Armstrong, when he took his first step on the moon, is supposed to have said, 'That was one small step for a man and one giant leap for mankind.' Years later he confessed his first words were 'Good luck Mr Jones!' because when he was a child he had an arrangement with his next-door neighbours, the Joneses, that if his ball landed in their garden he was allowed to go and collect it without asking for permission.

One evening he went to retrieve his ball and heard the Joneses shouting at each other through an open window. Mr Jones wanted sex and Mrs Jones didn't! She yelled, 'I won't have sex with you until a man walks on the Moon!' Armstrong didn't want to embarrass his old neighbours so kept what he really said secret until they were dead.

※ ※ ※

Sir Galbraith Lowry Cole G.C.B. fought in the Napoleonic Wars but missed the Battle of Waterloo because he was on his honeymoon at the time. In 1845 it was decided to build a monument celebrating his life. The area chosen used to be called Commons Hill, Camomile Hill, or Cow Hill. A fort was built there in 1689 by the then governor of Enniskillen, Gustavus Hamilton. In 1845 the area was enclosed, planted with trees, and transformed into a promenade and pleasure ground. Today Forthill Promenade and Play Park is a pleasant, 5¼-acre wooded park in central Enniskillen with shrub gardens, a children's play area and walks.

The monument took twelve years to complete. It is open to the public and contains 108 spiral steps, which lead to a viewing platform giving a spectacular view of Enniskillen and the surrounding countryside. The monument dominates the town.

※ ※ ※

A Russian gun, captured during the Crimean War, was brought to Forthill Park. In 1857 it was used to fire a salute marking the arrival of the first train in Enniskillen. The gun's reverberations broke the windows in Belmore Street.

❊ ❊ ❊

A solicitor called Terence Gibson appeared at Enniskillen Crown Court to represent a man who crashed into the back of his car. His defence was unsuccessful and his client was ordered to pay him £130.

❊ ❊ ❊

St Molaise is said to have brought soil containing blood from the early Christian martyrs from the Colosseum in Rome. He placed it on Devonish Island during the sixth century.

❊ ❊ ❊

People living around Lough Erne preserved their cots during the winter months by scuttling them. Cots are the only boat in the world to be treated in this way.

❊ ❊ ❊

Valentine Valentine came from Ballinamallard. He was born on St Valentine's Day.

❊ ❊ ❊

American President Bill Clinton's ancestral home is said to be in Roslea.

❊ ❊ ❊

Mahon's Hotel in Irvinestown has been visited by a surprising number of famous people, including the footballer Jack Charlton, Princess Anne's daughter Zara Philips, and two Secretaries of State

There's a presence in the room where I was born

for Northern Ireland, John Reid and Patrick Mayhew, the latter known for coming for the smoked eels! The hotel is the focus of the Lady of the Lake Festival and has been a family-run establishment for more than 125 years. Joe Mahon, the present owner, was born in what is now the residents' lounge. It is said to be haunted by a friendly 'presence', possibly the spirit of his aunt, who died there.

2

THE LAKELAND

There's an old saying:

> Lisnaskea, for drinking tea,
> Maguiresbridge for brandy,
> Lisbellaw for wrapping straw,*
> An' Enniskillen the dandy.
>
> (*making hay bales)

Things have changed since the above rhyme was written. Today Fermanagh caters for all tastes. There's a choice of outdoor pursuits, including canoeing, horse riding, cycling and walking. The scenery is spectacular. The Ardhowen Theatre is beautifully situated on the shores of Upper Lough Erne in Enniskillen and travelling up the Erne in a boat is a delightful way to visit. Amateur productions are often advertised throughout Fermanagh; the standard can be surprisingly high and the enthusiasm of the participants is contagious.

LOUGH ERNE

Lough Erne is the major feature of County Fermanagh. It's more than 40 miles in length and may be divided into two sections, Upper Lough Erne and Lower Lough Erne. The lough's names can be confusing because if you look at a page of a map on County Fermanagh, Lower Lough Erne appears above Upper Lough Erne. The reason is simple. In the past the whole of Ireland was united under the British Crown with Dublin as the capital city, and places were referenced regarding their proximity to the capital. 'Upper' indicates closer to Dublin so Upper Lough Erne is closer to Dublin than Lower Lough Erne. That rule applies to all Irish place names, for instance, Upper Ballinderry is marginally closer to Dublin than Lower Ballinderry.

The River Erne flows through Fermanagh. It begins in the Irish Republic in Lough Gowna, County Longford, and enters County Fermanagh via Upper Lough Erne. It is 152ft above sea level at this point. It then flows past Lisgoole Abbey and the Killyhevlin Hotel before swinging west and dividing into two strands, which go around Castle Island and Enniskillen. The two strands come together again at the Narrows, flow past Portora and on to Lower Lough Erne, 150ft above sea level.

In the 1830s, in an ordnance survey a royal engineer wrote, 'Lough Erne is navigable by barges and small craft throughout its whole extent, and presents by the magnitude of its waters, richly cultivated islands, sublime and diversified scenery, one of the most beautiful lakes in the world.'

That's still true. The lakes have become a major tourist destination, although Fermanagh has a damp climate so it's wise to bring stout shoes and good waterproofs.

I have had many enjoyable family holidays on Lough Erne, staying in one of the excellent hotels or bed and breakfasts. Hiring a cruiser also provides an excellent family break. Novices are welcomed and given a brief lesson on how to manage its vital equipment, such as the steering wheel and depth chargers. It's wise to follow advice given by instructors and insist everyone on board wears a life jacket at all times, except when bunked down for the night.

Navigation on Lough Erne is easy because painted, numbered markers have been placed near the water's edge around the lakes. The numbers tell you where you are. Plotting a route is similar to filling in a dot-to dot drawing. You simply use a map to work out where you want to go and follow the numbers to your destination. The markers are painted white on one side, red on the other. Keep to the white side. The red one indicates danger of running aground.

We loved breakfast on the lough with our cruiser surrounded by swans demanding to be fed. At night, after we had moored, we enjoyed craic in local pubs and/or with people tied up beside us. At the end of a week we were surprised to find we had only travelled a total distance of 5 miles!

Some people flash up and down the lakes as if there was no tomorrow. That's their choice and they undoubtedly enjoy the experience. Others simply want a restful holiday and savour every moment, walking, taking photographs, watching wildlife, fishing, visiting ancient monuments, doing rubbings of gravestones and other monuments as well as drawing and painting.

FISHING IN FERMANAGH

Upper Lough Erne is one of the best pike fishing lakes in Europe; it's possible to catch a specimen fish of between 20 and 30lb. There's no closed season for pike fishing but there is a bag limit. You must not catch more than one pike per day and all those weighing more than 4kg (approx. 8.8lb) must be returned to the water, alive and unharmed. Lures, spinners or dead bait trolled from a boat achieve the best results. Many fishermen, especially those from Germany, want to catch the biggest pike possible and so they come to the lough every year.

Lower Lough Erne is also famous for the mayfly fishing. The first mayfly is usually seen in early or mid-May and the season may continue on until late June. Dapping with a natural fly or dry fly fishing are the usual methods used.

Fishing begins in February with the arrival of the first salmon and grilse from May to July. There is wonderful trout fishing throughout the season.

Lough Melvin, at the western end of Fermanagh, has a run of grilse and spring salmon. It is home to three distinct species of trout, the gillaroo, the sonaghan and the ferox. The gillaroo is a particularly interesting fish because it tastes like chicken! An old folk tale says that when St Favor visited Lough Melvin she was immersed in a book and appeared distracted while seated at a table eating a meal. The local men thought: 'She's not concentrating on what she's doing! According to the rules of the church she's not allowed to eat meat on a Friday. She's supposed to be very holy!

Wouldn't it be the quare joke to see her breaking church rules by eating chicken!'

They put a plate full of chicken in front of her. The saint continued reading, but realised what they'd done. She was furious! She stood up, walked over to Lough Melvin and threw her meal into the lough's waters. The chicken turned into gillaroo trout and they thrived!

Trolling is the most used method for the spring salmon. Fly fishing for the sonaghan, gillaroo and grilse is excellent.

LEGENDS ABOUT THE ORIGIN OF LOUGH ERNE

The *Annals of the Four Masters* records ordinary events of life around the lough in the distant past. For instance, in 1397 Dermont O'Beirne caught a fever while he was away from home and his friends decided the best thing they could do was to take him home by boat. He became delirious, leapt into the lough and was drowned. The *Annals* also record legends about its origin.

Michael O'Clery, chief of the Four Masters, visited Lisgoole Abbey (Lios Gabhail), or the Abbey Church of Saint Peter, Saint Paul and Saint Mary, in 1631, the site of an old Irish monastery on the southern banks of upper Lough Erne. He stayed with some Franciscan brothers, who had been displaced during the Dissolution of the Monasteries and wrote a book, called the *Book of Invasions* (Leabhar Gabhála), recording some of the earliest legends about the origins of Lough Erne.

One legend says there once was a fierce battle against the Ernai, a sept of the Firbolgs, who lived on the plain now occupied by the Erne. The Ernai lost the battle and Lough Erne was formed by the water that flowed over them covering their remains.

The Reverend Henry Newland lived in Westbourne in Sussex. He loved fishing and spent many happy holidays in County Fermanagh. He recorded the following story about the origin of Lough Erne during the 1850s.

There once was a fairy spring hidden protected behind a large stone to keep it from being warmed by the sun. Local people knew it was important to keep the temperature and depth of the spring constant.

A young girl and her lover came to the well early one morning. She was thirsty so the young man rolled back the stone covering the spring and filled her pitcher with its cool, clear water. The young girl drank her fill and the couple began climbing up the cliffs. They forgot to replace the stone and the uncovered spring was left exposed to the heat of the early morning sun. Suddenly they heard a strange noise. They looked back. Water was boiling up from the spring below. It flooded the valley and an island, called the Eagle, or Erne rock, rose above the waters giving the Erne its name.

TRANSPORT AROUND THE LAKES

Some of the islands are still covered in the remains of ancient woodlands. The majority of Ireland's woodlands were cleared during the reign of Elizabeth I (7 September 1553–24 March 1603) to provide wood for the manufacture of ships and to make it more difficult for the native population using guerrilla tactics while attacking the queen's soldiers. Ulster was the last province in Ireland to succumb to Elizabeth's armies.

Wood from the original forests were used to make the first boats that sailed upon the Erne. They were simple oak dugout canoes formed by carving the central portion out of a large log. That is probably the type of craft in which early pilgrims travelled to the holy islands in Lough Derg.

The earliest log-boat found in Lough Erne was carbon-dated to 3520 BC. It became impossible to make dugouts after the forests were cleared and large oak trees were unavailable, and a tradition going back more than 5,000 years died out. Small boats, called 'cots', increased in number. They also have a long history going back more than 2,000 years. The Lough Erne Cot is unique because it is built to suit the watery conditions found locally. They varied in size, with a typical 'everyday' one 22ft long. Cots have flat bottoms and two ends that slope up, with each of these sections roughly the same size.

In 1850 Henry Newland, the fishing parson from Westbourne in Sussex (see previous section), wrote: 'The Erne is decidedly the best fisherman's river in Ireland, and can be equalled by few anywhere.' He realised poverty-stricken people in Fermanagh didn't regard fishing as a sport but as a means of getting something to eat and wrote: 'The salt eel is the staple food of Beleek and the favourite Lenten food of the Roman Catholics; and for this fish, the Erne is more famous than even for its salmon.'

He described cots as follows:

> The cot is a rough sort of boat, very much in vogue on Lough Erne. The whole lake is full of islands, some of which are very large, and many cultivated, and thus the cot is as necessary to these aquatic farms as a wagon would be to a farm on shore.

Cots! Huh! They look like deformed tablespoons!

Newland does not appear to have liked the cot's appearance because he continued, 'It is built somewhat in the form of an elongated tablespoon, with the handle off; it is of the rudest possible workmanship, frequently of unplaned planks nailed together and roughly caulked, but without the vestige of a keel.'

Cots took brides to weddings and corpses to funerals, as well as being used for fishing and wild fowling and to move livestock between the mainland and the islands. Sometimes the animals were put into a cot and sometimes they were tied on to ropes and made to swim across the water. Cots are very stable so could be used daily when cows on an island farm needed to be milked. It was possible to take buckets of milk across the water without spilling a drop.

It used to be possible, when walking along Lough Erne's shores, to see a cot completely submerged in water. That was how they were preserved.

COT RACING

Regular traditional cot races were held during the 1800s at Crom. Henry Newland described a cot's performance, writing:

> You would be surprised if you saw a Lough Erne boat-race; awkward and clumsy as it seems, if the day should happen to be perfectly still, it is the cot that invariably wins the race; their great broad flat frames seem to slip over the surface without touching it. But the slightest breeze is fatal to them; they drop to the leeward as unresistingly as a floating plank.

Lough Erne Heritage is a charitable organisation that aims to encourage local heritage research. Fred Ternan, of Lough Erne Heritage, who used to live on Inniscoornan Island (Inniscoorna means 'island of the sweet smelling flowers), said: 'Cots had disappeared completely from the lough. We felt that was a shame. The Heritage Committee decided it would be a good idea to build one. At first they thought they'd make a mock-up of ply wood just to show what it looked like, then they thought: "Why don't we build the real thing?" They contacted local people, such as John

Reihill, to find out as much about cots as possible. Luckily a local school teacher, Miss B. Beggin, known as Detta, had done a detailed drawing of a cot in the 1950s and it was used as a plan. Delta had since married and moved to England but she visited Fermanagh and approved of what they were doing. In 2016 they organised a project during which volunteers built two cots of the traditional length but 2in wider than usual so they could accommodate wheelchairs.

In May 2016 Lough Erne Heritage members decided to resurrect cot racing. Another cot was hurriedly built and finished a few days before the planned event. The first cot race for 100 years was held in August 2016 at Crom. The organisers recreated what is referred to as 'the famous cot race', which took place in 1856, at Crom. That race became famous because the crew's leader, John Goodwin, refused to take the prize money on behalf of the winning team. The team said they'd rather Lord Erne helped them arrange the return of their much-loved parish priest, Father Clarke, than win any amount of money! Father Clarke fled to America when he was warned he was going to be arrested for officiating at a mixed marriage. Lord Erne used his influence and was able to get the charges dropped. The priest returned to Fermanagh and ended his days in Newtownbutler.

The Lakeland Heritage cot race was a great success. John Goodwin's great-great-grandson, Michael Goodwin, took part in the race while the present Lord Erne, the great-great-grandson of the 1856 Lord Erne, gave out the prizes. Participants themselves said the race itself was 'mighty craic', but the best thing was having fun together, learning new skills and developing new friendships.

Cots were once used to transport heavy materials around Lough Erne. Transport cots were very different from racing cots and those in everyday use by farmers. They were larger and heavier, with some weighing between 16 and 20 tons. They usually had a mast and a sail, were fitted with four to six oars and their course was set by a paddle fixed to a pivot wheel. The largest cots were 50ft long, 10ft wide in the centre tapered to 3ft at each end, and were 5ft 6in deep. Even though they were very heavy, they had a shallow draft. Timber, iron, lead, coal and slates were imported through Ballyshannon, taken by horse and cart to Beleek and on to Enniskillen. Stone was carried from Carrickreagh quarry to Enniskillen and eels from the weirs at Killyhelvin to Belturbet. Portland stone used to build Castle Coole travelled to its destination in cots.

LIVING ON AN ISLAND

The Erne is a corridor valley formed during the Ice Age. As the ice retreated it left rounded mounds of earth called drumlins behind. They form small rounded hills with a characteristic rounded side facing the east and a longer, less steep incline on the west. The islands in Lough Erne are partially submerged drumlins. Once they were occupied but today few inhabitants remain.

Fermanagh people boast that there are 365 islands in Lough Erne, one for every day of the year. That's not correct, there are only 154: fifty-seven islands in the upper lake and ninety-seven in the lower.

Peggy Elliott was a colourful island dweller. She was born on Trasna Island in 1783. Her parents wrapped her in an orange flag and she was christened on the anniversary of the day King William of Orange won the Battle of the Boyne (12 July). The symbolism of the orange flag must have entered her soul because she became locally famous for her loyalty to the British Crown! She was given two nicknames, 'Orange Peg', and the 'Queen of Trasna'.

Peg lived a simple, hard life. One day a sudden storm blew up while her husband and two of her nine sons were out fishing. She watched helplessly as their frail craft foundered and they drowned. She lived to be 108 years of age and ended her life living with her 25-year-old granddaughter on the island. Peggy must have passed her loyalty to the British Crown on to her granddaughter, who was always dressed in orange and insisted on wearing green stockings so she could stamp on the colour of the opposition!

According to local historian, John Reihill, who once lived on Iniscorkish Island, fog frequently forms on the lakes around harvest time. He recounts a Saturday when his parents rowed across to the mainland to go shopping. A dense fog formed during their absence. At that time people called Lunny lived in the house closest to the lough. They had two collie dogs that barked noisily when anyone passed by. The Reihill children heard the dogs barking and told their granny. She made them go down to the shore and start beating a couple of empty tar barrels with sticks. They made a terrific racket, their parents heard it, headed towards the noise and reached home safely.

John recounted an experience of Packie Martin, from Innisturk. Packie and his brother, Phil, set out from Lisnaskea one night to return to their island home. There was a very dense fog. It didn't worry them because they had been out in pea-soupers like that in the past and they were sure they'd get home safely. They rowed and rowed, confident they were travelling in a straight line. There wasn't a star in the sky to guide them and eventually they began to suspect they were lost. Under normal conditions they expected to get sight of land in five to ten minutes, but none appeared. They stopped every now and again to see if they could hear some sort of a sound to help them get their bearings. They couldn't hear a thing so began shouting in the hope that someone would hear them. There was no response. After two hours rowing they sighted land and rowed ashore to find out where they were. They were at the Gullet at the back of Innisrooske, at least 3 miles off course in the wrong direction! They headed for home and, with careful navigation, eventually reached their destination by keeping the shoreline in sight as much as possible. It was a scary experience!

John says: 'Island dwellers know if you get lost in fog you're likely to do an about turn without realising it and you'll end where you started! If the fog is dense it's best for one person to row. That makes it easier to travel in a straight line.'

John and his wife, Sheila, loved living on Iniscorkish Island, but as they grew older he began to worry about the future. He said:

Island living is wonderful, but what happens when things go wrong? If one or other of us took ill how would we get a doctor? We hadn't any neighbours so there wasn't anybody who could help. It's not an ideal situation to leave a sick person on his/her own. I knew I could row Sheila across to the mainland if necessary but my strength would diminish with age. There'd come a time when I couldn't manage my cot. Sheila was born on the mainland and never could manage it.

Island living is expensive. We didn't have electricity so had to keep a reliable generator going. The generator needed diesel and oil. That had to be brought across to Inishcorkish by cot. I wasn't as fit as I was so was less able to row against a storm. I wondered what would happen on stormy nights on the lough if the cot's engine broke down? I could have been blown on to an uninhabited island and marooned. Eventually, we decided, with great regret, to sell our much loved home and move to the mainland. It broke our hearts, but it was the wise thing to do.

Sheila died in 2016. She was a lovely woman.

POITEEN (MOUNTAIN DEW)

Most of County Fermanagh consists of poor marshy land so farmers find it difficult, if not impossible, to make a living. Making and selling poiteen, a type of whisky, also called mountain dew, was one way they added to their income. Unfortunately distilling whisky is illegal. If people were caught by the revenue men their product was confiscated, their stills destroyed and they could be heavily fined or sent to jail, but, as the locals say: 'You have til live.'

Lough Erne's islands were once used to hide the illicit poiteen trade. There are so many it was impossible for the limited number of available revenue men to watch them all. The late Pat Cassidy, from Lisnaskea, told me the islands and cots were very useful in keeping the illegal manufacture of poiteen hidden. He said:

Many people living round the loughs learned how to row backwards. That meant you'd look as if you were coming and you were actually going! What you did was take the stuff to make a still out to an island in dribs and drabs. If you were stopped and searched you'd have nothing incriminating on you. When you got your all bits and pieces together you built a still and got tore into earning a living.

If you had a couple of dogs you could survive the coldest nights on one of the islands, especially if you found a stony piece of ground to lie on. Stones absorb heat during the day and give it out at night so they're a great place to lie down, much warmer than being on bare ground. Put a dog on your head and one

Poiteen's the quare stuff!

on your feet and you'd be as warm as toast. You could spend a
whole night dozing, keeping an eye on your still and still be alive
in the morning without suffering any of that auld hypothermia.

John McCollum of Pettigo, a pretty village that stands on both sides
of the border, said:

Aye, them revenue men go wild for poiteen! They once visited
a friend of mine. They searched his house from top to bottom,
so they did, but found nothing. They knew there was poiteen

somewhere but they couldn't find it! It was in the auld oil lamps scattered about the house! We'd a right laugh over that one, so we had. There are stiff penalties if you get caught, but sure that's just part of the fun.

SMUGGLING

Fermanagh shares a border with the Republic of Ireland and smuggling on both sides of the border was rife. Supplementing incomes by taking advantage of different prices on each side of the border was common practice, but the penalties, if caught, were severe.

Florence Creighton told me about a narrow escape her father, Jack Howe, had when he was smuggling piglets from the Irish Free State into Fermanagh. He crossed the border, went to Newbliss and bought sixteen fine little piglets from Tom McManus. They could only manage to pack eight little piglets into the van and set off for home. Unfortunately, Sergeant Shute, who was death on smugglers, had hidden on the border. He jumped out, got into the van and grabbed Jack's jacket. Jack slipped out of it, leapt out of the van and into the river along with the eight little piglets. His farm was on the border and he managed to get the piglets home. He was panic-stricken wondering how to get rid of the animals he'd bought; he hadn't anywhere to hide them. He knew Sergeant Shute would arrive as fast as his bicycle would carry him. If the piglets remained on his premises he'd be caught red-handed and would face an angry law! Luckily a neighbour, Benny Suzie, arrived in the nick of time, saw the piglets and was delighted to buy them. He walked them across Ernie Hall's field so Jack went scot free! Sergeant Shute hadn't any evidence to prove that anyone had been smuggling! Jack Howe was delighted because he'd sold the eight piglets for exactly what he'd paid for sixteen on the other side of the border. The only thing he lost from the whole deal was his old coat and he was thankful that, before setting out, he'd removed all signs of identification from his pockets.

Florence told me there were major differences in prices on both sides of the border, for example during the Second World

A wee bit of smuggling adds spice of life!

War tea was plentiful in Ulster and in short supply in the Irish
Free State.

John McCollum said:

Living here on the border that runs through Pettigo has both
advantages and disadvantages. Generally speaking shops in the
North are much cheaper than in the South. Sometimes it works
the other way, but I'd say nine times out of ten the North has the
best prices.

At the moment petrol is cheaper here, where we pay in euros. A lot of northerners come over to fill their tanks. During the summer the pubs are open for longer hours here than in the North. That means if you want to drink after hours you don't have to bother about closing time or being caught drinking illegally. You just walk up the street, cross the border and everything's hunky dory!

Smuggling's more or less a national pastime! If you have a friend on the other side of the border you can do profitable things with animals. Get them across and counted on that side, as well as here, and you can end up with two subsidies! That goes both ways.

I originally came from Portrush, but I married a wee girl from here. During the war I used to take a chance on the customs and fill the boot of my car with King Edward cigars. I made a fortune selling them up north. The customs men knew me. They thought I was just going home to visit my family. So I was, but I always made a profit on the trip.

Customs were annoying. They were just a money-making racket. When I got married I was given wedding presents. I had to declare them at the border and pay import tax on them or I could have been in trouble. I knew the custom official and he was decent. He only charged me £1 and gave me a receipt so they couldn't be seized in future. I thought having to pay anything was ridiculous!

Another annoying thing was they weren't manned twenty-four hours a day. They were manned from eight o'clock in the morning until eight o'clock at night. In the old days you had to get your book stamped going out of the country and coming back in again. If I was late returning I'd to get back first thing in the morning and never let on I'd been home, otherwise I was in dead trouble.

There's not as much smuggling as there used to be. The war was smuggling's heyday! There are severe penalties if you get caught smuggling, but sure, a wee bit of danger adds spice to life!

Today the pound sterling is the currency used in the north while the south uses euros. Sometimes it's very difficult to tell which country you are in. When I was in Pettigo I didn't realise I was in the south, went to pay for a cup of tea in sterling and was embarrassed when given a bill in euros. The waitress laughed. 'We take anything in the way of money! We even take pesetas!' The exchange rate given was one euro to one pound!

WARS IN LAKELAND

Lough Erne has a long history of being involved in wars beginning with the time of the Vikings when they swept up the lakes, in their longboats, during the ninth and tenth centuries. They were stopped at the mouth of the Erne in AD 830 but there was no effective resistance to later raids and none of the monasteries escaped.

In the seventeenth century the writers of the *Annals of the Four Masters* and the *Annals of Ulster* recorded Lough Erne as battle paths used whenever the Maguires, O'Neills and O'Donnells went cattle raiding.

Donn Carragh Maguire, who died in 1302, was the first Maguire family member to become chief lord, or prince, of Fermanagh. They managed to keep the title in spite of repeated attempts by the O'Neills and O'Donnells to overthrow them.

When Captain Cole became Constable of Enniskillen in 1607 he was made captain of the war boats and ended Maguire's supreme command of Lough Erne. He captured all Maguire's great boats to keep him from transporting animals he stole when cattle raiding. There is a picture map depicting the capture of the Maguires' castle at Enniskillen in 1593. It shows nine dugout canoes and three clinker-built 'great boats'.

Maguire got his revenge when he managed to steal two cots and a great boat from his old home.

More recently Fermanagh made a vital contribution to the Allied victory in the Second World War. (See Chapter 7 under Castle Archdale.)

FORESTS AND WILDLIFE

The lack of heavy industry in County Fermanagh allows the air to be free from pollution. Lichens are pollution indicators and shrubby lichens indicate very pure air. They are present in abundance. You don't see them very often now. In Fermanagh you'll find them growing in perfusion on the apple trees in Castle Coole and Florencecourt and to a lesser extent on other trees.

Vestiges of Ireland's original forest are found on some of Lough Erne's islands. They are mixed woods of oak, ash, elder, hawthorn, birch, hazel, holly, rowan, willow, blackthorn, apple and aspen. O'Hussy, a bard of the Maguires, used to sing of 'close-branched Enniskillen'.

There was an attempt at afforestation after the Second World War because growing trees answers many of Fermanagh's land problems. They give an inexhaustible supply of valuable raw material; they conserve water, protect the land from erosion and grow in poor soil. Conifers were widely planted because they are suited to the damp climate, peaty soil and are easier to get established in Ireland's windy climate.

Conifers have narrow leaves covered in a waxy substance, called the cuticle, that prevents water loss. Broadleaved trees lose a lot of water through their leaves and cannot survive in Ireland's wind without becoming established in shelter belts. Conifers are used to provide shelter for broadleaf trees, then removed once the broadleaved trees have become established.

Conifers have shallow roots that do not penetrate deep into the ground, and as a result they have a tendency to be unstable. They need to be planted close together to filter the wind, support each other and become more difficult to blow down. A single conifer is vulnerable in storms. One of the troubles of planting trees close together is that little light reaches the forest floor. Plants can't grow without light so conifer woods have little biodiversity.

Broadleaved trees have long tap roots to hold them in the ground and can survive once they become established. They lose their leaves in winter and the shadows they cast are not as dense as those under conifers so all sorts of plants can thrive underneath. In Fermanagh the uninteresting, sterile conifers are being replaced by broadleaved trees with a resulting increase in biodiversity.

Yellow Flag

The woods contain a profusion of sorrel, bluebells, ragged robin, enchanter's nightshade and so on, with violets, primroses and foxgloves around the edges.

The lough shores are thick with marsh marigolds, yellow flags, bog bean, cinquefoil, sedges, yellow and purple loosestrife and the common reed. The following plants that are comparatively rare in the British Isles grow in abundance on the shores of Upper Lough Erne – the blue marsh vetchling, the blue-eyed grass, the rare sea pansy and elongated sedge.

Fermanagh is unusually rich in mare's tail as nine of the possible eleven species of British ones grow there. Mare's tail is an ancient, primitive fossil plant that has existed on earth for more than a million years. It reproduces by spores, not seeds.

Bird watchers will find a lot to fascinate them around the Lakeland shores. Lough Erne isn't on any of the direct migration groups but the species that are present are varied and interesting. It is possible to see kestrels and sparrowhawks. The scoter, a black duck, which is predominately a sea duck, nests there. Coots and moorhens are plentiful, while terns nest at the mouth of the Erne at Belleek. There are large numbers of mallards, tufted ducks and golden eye ducks, while plovers nest at Rosscor. It is possible to see sandwich terns, black-headed gulls and lesser blackhead gulls, herons, cormorants and three types of swan; mute, whooper and Bewick's. The swans are easily identified because the mute has a neck that bends in a graceful curve, a beak that points downwards and a tail that points upwards. A whooper swan holds its head stiffly erect and its yellow and black beak is held parallel to the water as is its tail. Whooper swans do not breed on Lough Erne, they just visit the Upper and Lower Erne during the winter. Bewick's swans have beaks that are mainly black with a little yellow. They are rarer than the other types.

Tufted ducks are the most common type of duck found around the Erne and many of them nest on the shore. There are large numbers of cormorants, particularly on the lower lake. They are often found, sitting like ornaments, on top of the channel markers.

Herons are a common sight and often accompany boats travelling along the Erne. There surely can't be a more pleasant way to holiday than hiring a boat on Lough Erne and sailing with a heron for company.

3

SAINTS, SCHOLARS, HOLY WELLS AND ANCIENT STONES

Fermanagh has a spiritual atmosphere lingering from its past. It is a land of remains, the ancient remnants of religious beliefs embracing pagan practices as well as those of Christian origin.

The first people living in Fermanagh left traces of their existence, such as numerous raths, ancient stones, graves and circles. There's a Bronze Age stone circle on Boa Island and a cairn on Inishmacsaint. As a result there are so many ancient remains that there isn't space to include them all so described here are a few that should be particularly interesting.

RATHS

A rath is a roughly circular structure formed by high banks of earth and stone, sometimes with an associated moat. It is situated near water because water is essential for life. Sometimes a rath contained a building constructed of stone, in which case it is called a cashel.

Raths are often found in good defensive positions, usually on the top of a hill. They were once thought to have been built for defence. Today it seems more likely that they were farms.

Sometimes a church, monastery, or the king's dwelling was in the centre of the rath, so it would be protected by the circular bank. If the settlement was very large, so all the people associated with it could not be accommodated, outer circles were built around it.

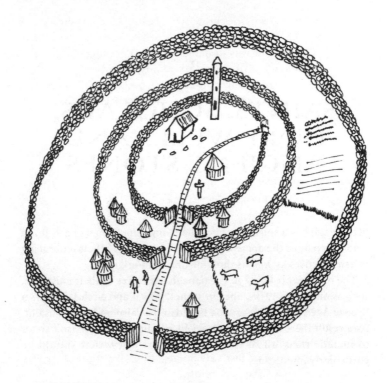

A Rath

Raths are almost impossible to date but some artefacts found in Fermanagh show they go back to the Bronze Age. They continued to be used until the twelfth century.

THE CELTIC CALENDAR AND ANCIENT BELIEFS

The old Celtic year celebrated four quarterly feasts, Lughnasa around 1 August, Samhain around 1 November, Imbolc around 1 February and Beltane around 1 May.

Our Christmas festivities grew from Imbolc, the ancient pagan mid-winter feast. Winter frightened primitive people because they believed the sun was in danger of disappearing completely. The religious leaders of the time (druids) worshipped the sun and designed rituals thought to keep it from disappearing. They believed their rituals caused the sun to come back, warm the earth and sustain life so they could continue to live on earth.

One of the customs associated with the festival was to collect holly and ivy and bring it indoors. These evergreens were thought to have the secret of eternal life because, unlike deciduous trees, they don't drop their leaves during the autumn and appear dead until the arrival of spring.

EARLY CHRISTIANITY

Irish Druidism absorbed some Christianity. As a result it's impossible to say when it ceased to be Druidism and became Christianity in a restricted sense of that term.

The old pagan feast of Beltane, which was held during springtime, was one of the pagan festivals adopted by Christianity. It was developed into our Easter celebrations.

Celts believed all wisdom comes from water. This led to the Christian practice of baptising an individual either by placing water on the head or by total immersion.

Rings, the Celtic sign denoting eternal love, are still used in marriage ceremonies because, as the Celts said, a ring is like eternal love in that it has no beginning and no end.

Lough Erne provided a highway along which Christianity could travel. It was used by pilgrims, saints, scholars and sinners, who passed along in sickness and in health from the earliest times, through the Middle Ages right up to the present. In 1407, a Florentine merchant on a Christian pilgrimage on his way to Lough Derg must have had contact with a local clergyman because he wrote: 'The said canon put me in a little boat, which was like a piece of roughly hewn hollow tree trunk.'

THE CULDEES

Joseph of Arimathaea was one of the first Christians to spread Christianity. He was a wealthy man, who lived in Jerusalem when Jesus was walking on earth. He was present at the Crucifixion, after which he asked for, and got, permission to intern Jesus's body in the unused tomb he had in his garden. He witnessed the Resurrection and, according to folklore, travelled to England and converted many people to Christianity. His followers became known as the Culdees. Some of them travelled across the sea and settled on Devonish Island.

The Culdees regarded themselves as the people of God, that is Ceile-De.

In some ways the Culdee version of Christianity is more like Protestantism than Roman Catholicism because members of the clergy were permitted to marry.

Culdees believe life is a journey from God, back to God again and that during life we should realise we are fused with the Divine Spirit. This belief is rooted in Gaelic Spiritualism. It respects Mother Earth and places unconditional love with God at its core. Culdees believe that consciousness of the Great Creator will, at worst, make individuals happy and at best prevent the gradual destruction of our world. They differ from other Christian groups of the time in that their monastic communities consisted of groups of detached huts or beehive cells and were not centred around a big cathedral as is the Roman custom, for example their settlement on Devonish Island does not have the remains of a large church.

The Culdee Church was 'the people's church' because it did not place much value on formal hierarchy. As a result when St Columban, a Culdee, wrote to Pope Boniface during the sixth century he wrote as a fellow bishop, not as somebody who felt he was in anyway inferior to the Roman Pope.

It is surprising how many well-documented arguments from the seventh century onwards between Culdees and Catholics foreshadow later Protestant–Catholic disputes.

Culdee monks living around Lough Erne were scholarly. They spent their lives making music, studying the scriptures and learning. The spread of their knowledge made Fermanagh become known as a county full of saints and scholars.

The Culdees were leaping around bare naked!

It has been suggested that St Patrick was a Culdee. There is no evidence that he visited Devonish Island but he is almost bound to have done so because the Erne was a major highway leading to Lough Derg, which is strongly associated with him.

St Patrick disagreed strongly with the then Pope, St Augustine, who had decreed individuals should pay the clergy to do their praying for them. St Patrick said people could access God directly and were quite capable of praying for themselves. That is the type of thinking adopted by the Culdees.

Culdees believed people should be given bibles written in their own vernacular language, which is very different from the beliefs of the Church of Rome. Eventually they annoyed the Church of Rome intensely because they didn't see any sense in paying dues to an organisation that they did not respect and to which they had no allegiance.

When St Bernard (1090–1153) was Pope he became angry when he learned the Culdees refused to go to Confession, pay tithes, or be married by clergy belonging to his Church. He said they were, 'beasts, absolute barbarians, a stubborn, stiff-necked and ungovernable generation, and abominable; Christian in name, but in reality pagans'.

At Easter Culdees living around Lough Erne stripped naked and were baptised by being completely immersed in the River Erne. Unfortunately the custom degenerated, tents were erected and they indulged in all sorts of sexual practices!

Over time the different Christian churches combined under the church St Peter founded in Rome. The Roman Church put great pressure on the Culdees to conform. The pressure eventually became unbearable so some of them gave in and merged with the Church, while many others escaped by emigrating to America.

ST PATRICK

County Fermanagh has many ancient places said to be associated with St Patrick, the patron saint of Ireland.

Several missionaries brought Christianity to Ireland before St Patrick arrived. They weren't well-organised but, as a result of their efforts, there were pockets of Christians living in separate unconnected groups throughout the island. What St Patrick did was make Christianity widespread and popular.

St Patrick found a mainly pagan society with its own deep-rooted traditions and customs. Instead of forbidding these old practices he adapted them to Christianity. It was much easier to change the meaning of pagan beliefs than to discard them.

The very early Christian Church was not a single entity because many of Jesus's disciples travelled away from Israel after the crucifixion. Each disciple shared his message and each individual had slightly different experiences. This gave rise to the foundation of many Christian churches, each one proclaiming slightly different versions of the same story, although the central message was both consistent and constant.

ST PATRICK'S HOLY WELL NEAR BELCOO

There is a beautiful holy well near Belcoo, once visited by St Patrick, for whom it is named after.

It can be difficult to find as roads starting in Fermanagh weave in and out over the border into the Irish Republic and southerners frequently do not signpost places on the other side of the border. However, people are very pleasant and friendly on both sides so there's no difficulty in asking for help. There is a signpost in the middle of Belcoo pointing to the road leading towards the holy Well.

The local authority on the well is Maíréad O'Dolan, who lives with her sister in the old station house on Garrison Road.

Maíréad wrote a marvellous book about the well and other stone monuments and church ruins in the neighbourhood called *Church Ruins and Stone Monuments near the Holy Well, Belcoo*.

Maíréad said: 'Tradition links St Patrick with the well. He gave it the ability to cure disease.'

According to Maíréad's book, her family have been herenachs (hereditary stewards of church lands) of Temple Rushin, the church associated with the holy well, for a long time. The church is now a ruin. One of her nephews, Cathal O'Dolan, his wife and family live nearby.

St Patrick's Well is beautiful. It has a lovely atmosphere and is larger than you may expect, about 20ft wide and 40ft long. It flows

Ye've come about four miles too far!

off into two rivers with an estimated yield of water of 600 gallons a minute. The locals say you can swim in it and in 1740 Isaac Butler described it as 'the best cold bath in the Kingdom, a spring exceedingly transparent and cold'.

Maíréad O'Dolan's book says: 'I have heard it said that the water is cold in summer and warm in winter. I have experienced wading in both seasons and know this to be true.'

The Ordnance Survey Memoirs of Ireland for 1835 states, 'the tradition of the olden times is that St Patrick sojourned in the parish for some time and that the holy well was an object of his peculiar favour as he endowed it with many miraculous privileges'.

In the past people walked long distances to visit the well and take water to cure loved ones. Its water has been credited for curing depression, stomach complaints, eczema and warts, among other complaints.

In 1739 Dean Henry, the Rector of Killesher, described the manner of bathing in the holy well as being indecent. He referred to drunkenness and debauchery, which caused the clergy to attempt to stop the pilgrimage. They didn't succeed, as recorded in the O.S. Memoirs of 1834:

> Some of the old inhabitants remember when the well was enclosed by a wall and had a small gate which was kept constantly locked and individuals who wanted to use the water were obliged to pay a small sum to the person who kept it. Doulagh Donagh (sic), or the last Sunday in July each year was the station day and crowds of diseased persons from every part of the country attended; and that the blind have received their sight and the lame thrown away their crutches at the well is attested by individuals residing in the neighbourhood.

Maíréad O'Dolan says the holy well is still used to cure people. She was once phoned by a woman who asked to be taken to the well because her son had committed suicide and she couldn't sleep. Even though it was outside the pilgrimage time Maíréad, the woman and her daughter made the stations. About a week later the woman phoned to say she could sleep again.

The correct way to do the stations is written on a leaflet, available in The Pilgrim's Manual, which may be found in the box attached to the fence or from the Leonard family. They live in the bungalow opposite the gate. It takes about an hour to make them.

In 1957 Father Leyden, the curate at the time, asked older people to record the prayers and the traditional way of doing the stations.

In April 2000 Father Ó Ríordáin thought it would be a good thing if people from all denominations could come and do the stations. He was asked to write alternative prayers for that purpose.

As a result the Pilgrim's Manual contains the traditional way (TW) and the alternative way (AW).

Every year a weekly pilgrimage to the well runs from the last Sunday in July until 15 August. It is advertised locally and people are available to lead the pilgrims.

In the past the pilgrimage was done in groups of twos and threes and that is still considered the best way.

The busy main road between Belcoo and Garrison is a hazard as it cuts across the path of the pilgrimage. Traffic warning signs are put in place and pilgrims are warned of the danger. Strong sticks are provided to help people's balance in, and around, the mill stream.

On many occasions the holy well has been in danger of extinction. One of the most serious threats was caused by the government during the years of the Great Famine (see Chapter 6). Road works were organised to provide work for the starving. Roderick Grey was the county surveyor for Fermanagh at the time and he had a fanatical belief that all roads should be straight and designed a road that cut straight through the middle of the holy well's site with a bridge over it. He would not change his mind; as far as he was concerned his road had to go over the well.

Local people didn't agree. They became very annoyed and used the cover of night to demolish work done during the day. Eventually Grey realised the road would never be finished if he didn't adjust his plans and the well was saved. The road goes round it.

A fair used to be held locally during the time of pilgrimage. Malachy O'Dolan told Maíréid there used to be twenty-three shebeens (illegal drinking dens, also called síbíns) at the fair. James Rogers wrote in the *Impartial Reporter* in 1926:

> Whiskey was cheap in those far off days as duty was low and the best of it, a native product, paid none at all; the licensed trade (to use the modern term) was fully represented in the form of numerous tents erected in the fair green, well stocked with liquor, warranted not to contain more than one headache a gallon.

> There was a class now almost extinct without which no fair years ago was regarded as complete. I refer to the travelling tinkers. Although no great respecters of laws, moral, religious or

civil, the tinker appealed to the Irish character largely because there was in the class something of the element of the picturesque and a great deal of the rollicking devil-may-care.

There was generally a little bloodletting before the fair was over; that goes without saying, for no fair was regarded as worth attending 100 or less years ago unless there was a little playful display with the blackthorn before its close. Indeed I have it on the best local tradition that there was a general belief amongst the full blooded men of the time that unless they had a certain amount of blood drawn periodically through the popular medium or otherwise their health would suffer.

Fifty years or so ago between 1st and 15th August pilgrims in quite large numbers, many from a considerable distance, attended to make the stations as it was termed; but to show the changes which time brings about in so many ways, the stations is but a mere shadow of what it was half a century ago.

The Belfast antiquarian Francis Joseph Bigger visited the holy well and was upset when he saw the neglect it had suffered. He wrote a letter to the *Impartial Reporter* that was published on 11 September 1913:

Vandal minds and destructive hands planned and laid the new road right through the sacred spot, breaking up the old paths and dividing the stations, injuring the well, just as they wished to break the old faith and ancient rites ... Surely now, however a better era is dawning and the church of the holy well, the church of St Patrick, will yet be saved as the most sacred and lovely thing in the parish of Cleenish?

Tradition says the old people ignored the church's disapproval and continued to make the stations. They still do today, although not in as great numbers as in the past.

It's a beautiful place, with roots reaching back into Ireland's pagan past. Over the years it has been changed into a Christian site and it is well worth a visit, even if you do not make the stations of the Cross.

**I'm telling ye, holy wells shouldn't be neglected!
Frances Joseph Bigger said so!**

DEVONISH ISLAND AND
ROUND TOWERS

Devonish Island is very peaceful and easy to visit, either by taking
an organised boat trip from Enniskillen or by hiring a cruiser and
going there yourself.

If you have hired a cruiser and want to land on Devonish make sure to moor on the side of the island where you can see the round tower and the ruins of an old church with its associated buildings. The other side of the island contains a field of very ferocious cows, which once attacked a woman taking her dog for a walk and killed the animal.

When on Devonish Island look for carved heads among the ruins. Look carefully at the little church, known as St Molaise's house after its founder. It has foliage designs carved around the bases of its angles. If possible, climb up to the top of the round tower. It was built during the twelfth century and has a marvellous view from the top. It is well worth the climb.

There is a theory that round towers were used as lookout stations as part of the defence strategy against marauders, such as the Vikings. A monk was thought to be posted as a sentry at the top of the tower. If he saw the threat of an attack he warned the other monks. They grabbed their valuables, used a ladder to climb up to the door, pulled the ladder up behind them and stayed there until it was safe to come down again. However, that is probably wrong. If the monks retreated inside a round tower the marauders would have found a way to reach the wooden door and set it on fire. The thin wooden floors inside a circular structure would have caused the tower to behave like a chimney and the monks would have been smoked out.

Another theory about round towers is that they acted as a status symbol for the monasteries erecting them. They could be seen from afar and would proclaim the presence and wealth of the organisation that built them. That doesn't make a lot of sense either because boasting about wealth and advertising presence would be bound to invite attack from invaders such as the Vikings.

The Irish name for round tower is bell tower and that was probably their main purpose. A hand bell could have been rung from the top window to summon the monks for services and so on. A place of storage and defence was probably a secondary purpose.

The method used to build round towers is interesting. A cord was tied to a stick and used to draw a circle in the same way as we would use a set of compasses today. That gave the basic shape and building continued from there.

At the little church on Devonish all the monks had jobs. St Molaise wrote, or copied, beautifully illustrated books. Folklore says he became tortured by the voices of ghosts from his past. He knew the best way to deal with ghosts is to face them, so, on a clear moonlit night he stood on Devonish's shore and challenged the ones who were haunting him to appear. To his horror phantoms

Why can't I write?

from his past, including those of his parents and the girl to whom he had once been betrothed, rose out of the depths of the lough and came towards him. He believed his soul was in danger of being lost forever and was terrified. He dropped down on his knees and prayed, as he'd never prayed before, for salvation. He was saved when the first light of dawn touched the shore where he was kneeling and the phantoms vanished.

St Molaise was so badly shaken by the experience he couldn't write but be became inspired to produce sculptures. According to folklore, many of the ancient sculptures in County Fermanagh are his work, but his mind was damaged by his experience. As a result some of his sculptures were so obscene they were either hidden, or destroyed, by monks.

SHEELA-NA-GIGS AND OTHER ANCIENT STONES

A Sheela-na-gig is a carving of an extremely ugly woman, with an agonised look on her face and her hands holding her private parts. She is said to be in the process of giving birth and is an ancient fertility symbol. In the past local women often went to be near a Sheela-na-gig when experiencing a difficult labour. They believed she would help them.

Carvings of Sheela-na-gigs may be either free standing or carved into the wall of the church. Wooden or stone ones were once present in all churchyards. The wooden ones have decayed and disappeared, but many of the stone ones have survived.

A Sheela-na-gig sometimes has what seems to me a peculiar effect on some women. I once saw a woman, who looked eccentric, rather like an old-style hippy with long flowing hair, robes and earrings, rush towards the Sheela-na-gig in the now defunct History Park in County Tyrone, fling her arms around it, cry, 'Mother!' and burst into tears as she clung to it.

WHITE ISLAND, NEAR DEVONISH

White Island, near Devonish, used to be called Inishcomheata Island, meaning 'island of the watching or guarding'. It was under the precincts of the monastery on Devonish and its ancient church was used by St Comgall of Bangor as a place of retreat. He died in AD 602. He must have been a harsh man because he believed in mortifying the body and insisted that he and his monks lived a very spartan life. The lifestyle was so hard that seven of his followers died.

SAINTS ASSOCIATED WITH INISHMACSAINT

Inishmacsaint means island of the plain of sorrel. It, like many of the other islands, has a rath. It also has an ancient cross that tradition says rotates three times to the rising sun on Easter Sunday morning.

According to folk tradition, the sun is so happy to remember that Jesus rose from the dead that it dances every Easter morning. As a result, no matter how cloudy and dull Easter Morning happens to be you can, according to folklore, always get a reflection from a shiny surface, such as a spoon.

Inishmacsaint was the site of a monastery founded by St Ninnidh. He was nicknamed 'Saebhruise', which means one-eyed. The oral tradition says he was educated at Clonard, under St Finian, along with St Molaise of Devonish, St Ciaran of Clonmacnois and St Maedoc (Mogue) of Ferns. That yarn is hard to credit because of the difference between the saints' ages.

St Ninnidh is said to have been one of the twelve clerics fed on the milk of St Ciaran's dun cow. After the cow died her hide was used to make parchment. St Ciaran lent St Ninnidh a book made from her skin, saying: 'I know her hide will return to me.'

Incidentally, the Book of Kells, which is held in Trinity College Dublin, is reputed to have been written on parchment that came from the dun cow's hide. It must have been a very big cow!

St Ninnidh travelled along the south shore of Upper Lough Erne, preaching as he went. He is said to have fasted during one Lent beside the upper lake on Knockninny Hill, which is named after him. It probably was a pagan site he felt needed to be 'Christianised'. Prehistoric remains still exist there.

St Ninnidh arrived on Inishmacsaint in about AD 530. His monastery never became either rich or famous. It is surrounded by a rath of mixed earth and stones, which is still traceable.

The church on Inishmacsaint is a ruin. It is surrounded by a circular graveyard, which is a sign of its Celtic origins.

During St Ninnidh's lifetime it was customary for ecclesiastics to make a pilgrimage to Rome. While he was doing that he was called back to see St Brigid, who was dying and he anointed her on her deathbed.

Senach, the saint-smith of Derrybrusk, County Fermanagh, gave St Ninnidh a bronze bell. It was kept in the parish church until the seventeenth century, after which it was held in Castle Caldwell's museum. Now it is in the National Museum of Scotland.

SCULPTURES ON WHITE ISLAND, IN CASTLE ARCHDALE BAY

White Island, in Castle Archdale Bay, is one of the most interesting islands and has a fine rath. The origins of White Island and its original name are lost in the past; it could be called after an ancient yew tree, the name coming from Eo-inis (yew tree island).

The Register of Clogher records that Bishop Matthew Casey went to the church of St Constans in Eo-inis to take the relics of St Constance to Clogher Cathedral. Tradition says it was founded by St Patrick in AD 409. The relics were placed in the shrine the saint had presented to St Macartin and are now in the National Museum in Dublin. It has been suggested that the figure found on the island in 1958 represents St Constans.

The island has the remains of a small church with a Hiberno–Romanesque doorway. The church has been dated to the late twelfth century. Perhaps the most fascinating features of White Island are the eight socketed stone figures discovered on the island at various times. It is thought these ancient figures were originally used as building stones because they have sockets in their heads. At least five of them were built into the church on the island. It has been suggested that they were built into the church because they were sacred and being part of the building ensured their survival. The same thing was often done with Anglo–Saxon crosses.

The croziers carried by two of the figures resemble the crozier shrines of the ninth to twelfth centuries. The door has been dated as twelfth century so the carvings are older than the church. One of these figures is thought to be a nobleman because it wears a brooch, known as a penannular brooch. That type of ornament was not made after the tenth century so perhaps the figures predate the door by at least two centuries.

The similarity of style and type of stone used suggests the figures were carved at the same time, possibly by the same hand. An unfinished stone had been abandoned because it contained a fault, so it is possible they were carved on the island. The sculptor who carved them was very skilful because they are beautifully modelled. They have smooth surfaces, which contrast with the crisply carved details of the clothes, faces and hair. They show no sign of emotion or movement; their eyes are round and stare fixedly ahead with their mouths forming a stylish pout.

Two of the figures must be clergymen because they carry a crozier and one also has a bell. The nobleman with a brooch also has a sword and a shield. The statues are wearing the same type of upper-class dress consisting of a cloak over a long tunic.

Nobody knows for certain who these figures represent or why they are on White Island. It has been suggested the figure with its left hand raised to its mouth may be St Patrick while the curly haired pair could be King Leary and his son Enna. Legend says St Patrick raised them from the dead.

The original use of the sculptures is not known. Six of them can be paired according to their height and all of these ones have a socket carved into the top, apparently to support wooden beams. It has been suggested that these could have been used as supports for three wooden steps leading to, say, a pulpit or an altar.

The beaked quadrupeds are curious creatures similar to those found in the Lindisfarne Gospels, which was illuminated by Eadfrith around AD 700. He had been trained in Ireland.

It is thought that the figure, found at the base of the south wall in 1958, represents a woman. According to local tradition nuns once lived on the island. This statue is wearing a scalp-covering cap and a veil, that and its open mouth and tongue could denote female characteristics.

The Sheela-na-gig on White Island, if that is what she is, is unusual because she is wearing a cape. She has bulging cheeks and wide mouth and was carved in Ulster. There was a taboo, recorded in Ulster saga, forbidding men to look at women's breasts. As a result women exposed their breasts and were sent out to the front of battle lines so the enemy would avert their eyes!

Similar figures to those found on White Island are found at Carndonagh in Donegal and Killadeas in Fermanagh. This fact may hint that there was once a tradition of stone carving that was restricted to the western section of Ulster.

Tradition states the Church of Ireland Cathedral in Armagh was founded by St Patrick and pagan stone figures were once built into its walls. These figures were scattered and rediscovered during the nineteenth century while the cathedral was being restored. Since then most of the pagan figures have been returned to the precincts of the cathedral as they are part of its history. Perhaps the same sort of thing happened on White Island?

BOA ISLAND AND JANUS FIGURES

Boa Island (pronounced 'bo') is the largest Island in Lough Erne. It is called after Badhabha, one of the three Celtic war goddesses, the other two being Macha and Morrigan. Badhabha means 'battle fury' or 'carrion crow'. The three goddess appear to have been interchangeable.

Badhabha had a special connection with childbirth so is both a destroyer and a creator, a goddess of war and a mother goddess. Celtic goddesses were not territorial; they didn't belong to a particular tribe.

Boa Island is situated approximately 15 miles from Enniskillen on the road to Kesh. It is very narrow and is approximately 5 miles in length. It's very accessible because the main A47 travels along its

Janus figure on Boa Island

length. The island is joined to the mainland by two bridges, one at the west side on the part of the road leading west towards Castle Caldwell, the other at the eastern end towards Kesh. The first time I travelled along it I didn't realise I was on an island! It was raining at the time and visibility was poor.

Cladragh Cemetery, on Boa Island, contains two interesting Janus figures. A Janus figure is one with a head and a body on two sides. These figures are easily reached because the churchyard is only a short walk from a very minor road that runs directly off the main road. It is clearly marked.

Two other easily reached Janus figures are in a graveyard at Killadeas, near the Manor House Hotel. Killadeas got its name from the Culdees (Ceile-De), of Devonish, who once owned the land. (Kil, or Cil, in a place name means it was the site of an ancient church.)

IMPORTANCE OF THE HEAD

The head was a very important symbol to the Celts, who looked upon it as the seat of the soul, a symbol of the life force and power of the Other World. The east face of the Boa figure has remnants of horns. A horned or antlered head was thought to be especially powerful. It also has bared teeth, clenched fists and what is probably a phallus so it could be a hermaphrodite cult figure with bisexual fertility powers, as well as the supernatural ability to look in both directions.

Another theory is the figures are idols belonging to refugees from ancient Roman Gaul. Etruscans believed in life after death and thought that making stone images of their ancestors could ensure fertility and success in war. Sculpting stone monuments of two-headed Janus images was an Etruscan practice.

FOLKTALE ABOUT THE ORIGIN OF JANUS FIGURES

An old folk tale about the origin of Janus figures tells of a time long ago when wizards lived on an enchanted isle in the middle of the Atlantic Ocean and worshipped the goddess Danu.

The Atlantic Ocean loved the goddess and became very annoyed with the wizards for wasting their magic on trivial things that polluted the environment. Eventually he became so cross he decided to destroy them, but the goddess intervened. She said: 'Stop and think. If all the wizards disappear nobody will know of their existence. Nobody will learn how they went wrong and nobody will learn from their mistakes. Please let some of wizards survive.'

The Atlantic Ocean thought about what the goddess said and decided to allow thirty wizards to escape in silver boats and sail to his fringe. Some landed in South America, others reached Europe and one arrived on the beautiful green island we now know as Ireland. The Atlantic Ocean created a gigantic earthquake that drowned the wizards remaining on the isle and buried it beneath his depths. It is said the place where the island once was is now known as the Bermuda Triangle and the story explains why heads found as remnants of Aztec culture on the other side of the Atlantic Ocean resemble those found in County Fermanagh.

THE DIPPERS

In the 1920s an obscure sect of Protestants, called the Dippers, was formed. They believe the Erne to be the true River Jordan and baptise their members in it.

THE OLD PLACES

Folklore refers to ancient monuments as the 'old places'. It was once thought dangerous to go anywhere near them at night because the fairies might steal you! They really do have a magical, mystical, other world feeling that has to be experienced to be believed. It's as if the spirits of people who lived and worked there in the past have in some way been transmitted into the surrounding earth.

4

THE BIG HOUSES

CASTLE COOLE

Lough Coole has a crannog and is surrounded by the Killynure Hills. Castle Coole is called after Lough Coole, which comes from the Irish Gaelic word cúil meaning 'seclusion'. Its very seclusion explains how so many old oak trees escaped being cut down and used to build sailing ships during the reign of Elizabeth I.

A crannog is an artificial island usually formed by hammering pointed wooden piles into shallow water in the shape of a circle. The shape was filled in with rocks, stones, earth and anything else available. If wood wasn't available the structure was made out of anything at hand. They were used as dwelling places.

There are two other lakes, Lough Yoan and Brendrum Lough in the grounds of Castle Coole. The property was bought by a Belfast merchant, John Corry, in 1656. He was the grandfather of the first earl.

Castle Coole has been described as 'a castle in a park'. It's a beautiful house built by two architects of the Georgian period. Richard Johnston, who was Irish, originally received the commission. He laid out the ground plan and completed the basement before being replaced by the then fashionable English architect, James Wyatt. Wyatt didn't start afresh; he simply used Johnston's footprint and designed the mansion in neoclassical style. The English artist, Joseph Rose, is responsible for the fine, varied plaster ceilings in the house.

Castle Coole was transferred to the National Trust in 1951 by the 7th Earl Belmore because the 5th and 6th Earls of Belmore died within eighteen months of each other. They didn't have any children and the property was faced with horrendous estate duties. It's an unusual stately home because its contents have remained intact. They belong to the 7th Earl of Belmore and can be seen by visitors today. The earl lives in a small house on the estate and has an apartment in one of the wings, which is used by his heir's family.

The house has a State Bedroom which was furnished, complete with a magnificent bed, for an expected visit by George IV. Unfortunately after disembarking at Dublin the king went to Slane and was introduced to a very attractive young lady so he never got as far as Castle Coole.

Alan Heuton, the head gardener says:

> The Earls of Belmore, who owned Castle Coole, were good landlords. They were respected and loved by their tenants. Whole families were employed here for generations. Tenants were provided with good wages, good quality housing and fuel. They were allowed to burn fallen branches from the estate's woodland, but weren't allowed to touch a living tree. They used to secretly hammer stones into the places where tree branches joined the trunk. The limb became weak and eventually fell to the ground so it could be used as fuel!

CHABAL, THE GIANT OAK

Chabal is a giant oak tree hidden in a quiet corner of the estate. It is the estate's oldest and biggest tree, measuring 25ft around the trunk. Alan says: 'A tree's age can be estimated by measuring its circumstance 4ft above the ground. Every inch equals a year. Therefore 25ft, which is 300in, equals 300 years. In other words Chabal is older than the house! A visitor, who was a tree expert from Kew Gardens, suggested Chabal was even older because similar giant oaks had been shown, by carbon dating, to be more than 500 years of age.

Chabal has been lucky to survive for so long. Alan pointed out the shape of its magnificent branches and the angle at which they go in the trunk and said:

In the past branches like that were used to form the prow of ships. It's the ideal shape. Oaks are very strong. Their branches have strong tubular structures passing from the tree's roots to its furthermost tip. The tree uses them to carry water. A prow made from branches that shape will inherit the oak's strength and will

Boys-a-dear! Yon's some tree!

be excellent for ramming enemy ships. I reckon the only reason Cabal [*sic*] survived is that it's tucked away in a quiet, inaccessible corner of Fermanagh.

Oaks produce a natural wood preservative, called tannin, which enables them to survive intact for 1,000 years. Tannin is very useful; it is used to preserve animal skins so they can be turned into leather jackets, coats, shoes, handbags and so on.

Whiskey must, by law, be matured in oak casks for at least three years. The oak is what gives the famous dram its flavour and colour. Whiskey is Britain's third largest export and its popularity is due to the oak.

The oak has been described as being the 'corner stone' of the forest ecosystem. One oak tree can support more than 1,000 species of flora and fauna. That's why an oak leaf is the symbol of the National Trust.

The remains of an old coach road run through the estate. It is bordered by magnificent oaks, but they are not equal to Chabal.

One local resident, Hugh Mills, loved walking through Castle Coole's magnificent grounds with his wife Lara and their small poodle. Unfortunately, Lara developed cancer and died. As she became weaker she could only walk as far as a seat beside the drive before taking a short rest and returning home. Hugh asked if he could plant a tree in her memory but Alan had to refuse because he receives many similar requests. However, he suggested the National Trust, as part of its tree-planting programme, could plant a sequoia for Lara, which it did. It is thriving and is growing into a beautiful shape. On 23 June 2010 Hugh wrote a letter of thanks saying:

> We had a lovely day at the end of May for friends and family when we met at the end of May.
>   I will watch with interest hopefully for a number of years how the tree develops. The location you chose is very appropriate given that Lara would walk her dog and maybe take a short rest on the seat opposite before heading back to Castle Wood.

Alan Heuton's attitude is typical of people employed at Castle Coole. He said:

I look upon the grounds of Castle Coole as my own farm. When I'm off duty say at weekends I feel uneasy unless I have to go and see how 'my land' is doing! My wife says I've the Castle Coole disease and it's wonderful to know all the members of my family have caught it! I love to see and hear them doing holiday jobs here, such as acting as guides.

FLORENCE COURT

There is a close connection between Castle Coole and Florence Court, another beautiful stately home in Fermanagh belonging to the National Trust. It, like Castle Coole, is loved by the people who work there and is set in spectacular grounds. One feels one could live there, which is a rare feeling to have in a National Trust property. The rooms have a friendly, lived-in atmosphere and they aren't too big; they look comfortable and cosy.

Florence Court features exquisite plaster decoration and some fine Irish furniture. It is well worth a visit, as are the grounds, although Heather Hamilton, the Education Officer, says Florence Court is built on an ant hill as she has never seen so many ants anywhere!

Heather tells an interesting story about Benaughlin Mountain, which towers above the house and is referred to as 'Bin Mountain' by locals. The name Benaughlin comes from the Irish, Binn Eachlabhra, meaning 'the peak of the speaking horse'. Apparently there is a rock formation on the side of the mountain away from Florence Court, that looks like a horse rearing up. A local landlord used to tell people if they were bad the horse would come and get them!

Another legend says a large, white horse used to appear on Benaughlin's slopes during the last Sunday of July every year and talk to local people.

The influence of the family who once lived in Florence Court is very evident; for instance there is a bookshop called Nelly Wooly Bookshop. Nelly Wooly was a favourite family dog; it was buried in the grounds and her grave is marked on a map of the property.

The first house on the site was built by John Cole (1680–1726). He named it after his wife, Florence, but waited until after her death before he gave it her name!

An anonymous history of Fermanagh, written in 1718, described Florence Court as being 'very costly and sumptuous'. In 1739 the Reverend William Henry described the house as 'small, being only the left wing of a grand building'.

It is thought the house was built in at least two stages because the rich rococo plasterwork in the dining room, drawing room and

Nelly Wooly

stair hall are of a later date than the baroque plasterwork in the study and library at the front of the house. Also, the floorboards in these two rooms differ in width from those of the rest of the house.

John Cole's son, Lord Mount Florencecourt, held a large housewarming party there in 1764. It's logical to think the reason for his party was that he'd extended his house and wanted to show it off.

The 5th Earl of Enniskillen wanted to make sure the property survived intact so transferred it, along with 14 acres of land, to the National Trust in 1953. He couldn't manage the escalating costs of keeping the house and estate in good repair because the 1950s and '60s were a bad time for the family. Their income was decimated after the Second World War when the price of agricultural produce plummeted.

In 1955, an electrical fault in the hallway at the top of the stairs leading to the first floor caused a devastating fire that destroyed the upper rooms of the building. The 5th Earl of Enniskillen was in Belfast at the Ulster Club when the fire was discovered by Lady Enniskillen. She ran downstairs to the servants' quarters and raised the alarm.

At that time telephones were rare. Florence Court didn't have one so Lady Enniskillen rushed to nearby Killymanamly House, which had a telephone. She rang her elderly husband and exclaimed: 'The house is on fire!' He yelled: 'What the hell do you think I can do about it?'

Fire brigades had the fire almost under control by 9 a.m., but dry weather conditions helped to reignite the blaze. The flames reached the roof of the building and caused it to crash down into the hall. By the evening about two-thirds of Florence Court's interior was in ruins.

The firemen quenched the flames by using gallons of water, which caused a lot of damage but there were a couple of lucky escapes. Violet Grosvenor, who later became the Duchess of Westminster, saved the exquisite ceiling in the dining room. She saw it was in danger of collapsing because water was accumulating above and it was beginning to bulge. She asked two local builders, Bertie Pierce and Ned Vaughan, to drill six holes in the flat part of the ceiling. That action allowed the water to escape and saved it. Two of these holes can still be seen today.

Plasterwork above the original staircase was soaked by water from the firemen's hoses, which saved the staircase by falling on top of it. As a result Florence Court still has its original magnificent staircase.

Furniture and paintings were removed, some by being thrown out of windows. A bust of King William III, locally referred to as 'King Billy', had the nose damaged when it fell flat on its face.

Sir Albert Richardson was put in charge of the restoration of Florence Court, which has been returned to its former glory although some of the rooms on the upper floors are still closed.

The Cole family had another disaster in 1956 when their only son and heir, Michael, Viscount Cole, died suddenly. He was only 36 years of age and wasn't married. Then, in 1961, just as restoration of the house was nearly finished, Hurricane Debbie devastated the estate and in 1962 the 5th Lord Enniskillen and his wife died within three months of each other.

Captain David Lowry Cole, M.B.E. (1918–89), became the Rt Hon. the 6th Earl of Enniskillen. He was the 5th Earl's nephew. David (as he was popularly known) had spent much of his life in Kenya. He and his first wife, Sonia, had two children, a son and a daughter. He and Sonia were divorced so his second wife, Nancy, became the Countess of Enniskillen. They lived in the house until 1973 when, at the height of the Troubles they moved to Scotland (Kinloch House, Kinlock, Perthshire). The earl and his wife took most of the original furnishings with them. The Dowager Countess of Enniskillen left most of the furniture to Florence Court on her death in 1998 and it returned home.

David was the last Earl of Enniskillen to live in Florence Court. His son Andrew became the 7th Earl of Enniskillen when his father died in 1989. He lives on a vast estate in Kenya.

FLORENCE COURT'S FOSSIL FISH COLLECTION AND LONDON'S NATURAL HISTORY MUSEUM

When he was very young, William Willoughby Cole (1807–86), who became the 3rd Earl of Enniskillen, became addicted to collecting fossils. Eventually he decided to specialise in collecting fossil fish and to set up his own museum in Florence Court. He chose the South Pavilion at the end of one of the wings and decided to do the job properly with light provided by a glass lantern roof. His father objected because he thought collecting fossils was 'a waste of money' and 'damned nonsense'.

However, the young viscount didn't let his father's opinion deter him. He was rightly proud of his collection and wanted to show it off to his friends, so he invited them to stay. He hoped his distinguished guests would impress his father, and they did. The old lord withdrew all opposition and the young viscount was able to finish building his museum the way he wanted. He displayed his collection in glass cases and his enthusiasm for fossil fish never failed. His collection became one of the largest and most scientifically important collections of fossil fish in private hands anywhere in the world. Eventually he owned nearly 10,000 individual specimens. His collection stayed in Florence Court until he transferred it to the Natural History Museum in London, where it is still a prized research collection.

CROM CASTLE

Crom Castle is up a narrow, twisting road along which it feels as if every tree, every flower and every stone has a story to tell. The castle looks like one out of a fairy tale, but unfortunately it's not open to the public. It's near the site of the old castle, which was built by John Creighton when he settled in Fermanagh during the early seventeenth century.

John Ynyr Burges of Parkanaur, County Tyrone, stayed in Crom Castle in 1863 and wrote in his diary: 'There is no place that conjures up in my mind more Irish romance than the wide and fair domains of Crom.' That is still true today. The grounds are a nature reserve and there's a delightful nature display in the information centre as well as a tea room, and the site contains excellent self-catering tourist accommodation.

In 1689, David Creighton, one of John Creighton's descendants, successfully defended the family seat against an attack by a large body of James II's army. The young Creighton made a sally just as a corps of soldiers from Enniskillen approached to relieve the castle. As a result the besiegers were caught between two lines of fire, which resulted in terrible slaughter and caused Lough Erne to turn red with blood.

The number of soldiers killed on that day gave estate workers a nasty shock several hundred years later! There is a ring of trees, known as the Fairy Ring, near the old castle. Some estate workers wanted gravel to use on the paths on Crom and they knew it was easy to dig the soil in the Fairy Ring. They began digging and found human bones, upon which they quickly replaced the earth and asked for expert advice. They were told that in the past so many soldiers were killed in battle it was impossible to give them decent burials. The bodies were gathered up and put in a communal pit with a ring of trees planted around them to mark the spot and ensure they were not disturbed again.

CROM'S FAMOUS YEW TREES

Two magnificent yew trees were planted at the gate of the original castle. They are more than 800 years old and said to be the oldest in Ireland. According to local legend, Lord O'Neill said goodbye to his lady love under their branches at the time of the 'flight of the earls'.

THE HA-HA

The ruins of the old plantation castle are situated near Lough Erne's shore along with traces of a late seventeenth-century formal garden and a bowling green enclosed by a ha-ha. A ha-ha was built on many of the old estates because their owners had a lot of animals and didn't want them traipsing all over their nice gardens. Fences spoil the view so the ground at the end of the garden was raised to a much higher level than the ground below. A sort of wall was formed that couldn't be seen from the house. It was called a 'ha-ha' because if an unsuspecting visitor fell from the lawn into the field below everyone laughed, 'ha-ha'!

CROM'S GHOSTS

The present-day castle is nearby, on elevated ground. It was built in the 1830s for the 3rd Earl of Erne and was designed by the architect Edward Blore, who was responsible for sections of Buckingham Palace. It looks grand and a bit spooky. Sharon Sey, who works in the information centre at Crom, says it is haunted.

I'm telling you, I saw a white lady!

She said:

> A party of Americans stayed for a fortnight in Crom Castle and
> remarked that it is very haunted. They felt a presence and heard
> all sorts of noises like footsteps in corridors and doors shutting.
>
> Violet Johnston used to work in the castle. She once saw a
> white lady standing beside a table, brushing her hair with a sliver
> hairbrush. She sat down and disappeared. Violet wondered if
> her eyes had been deceiving her and walked over to look at the
> table where she'd seen the lady. It was covered in dust apart from
> the place where the lady had been sitting, which looked highly
> polished and there were hairs on the hair brush.

Sharon also told me her father was once driving his car down a road
near Crom when an evil-looking woman appeared in front of him.
She gave him a nasty look and disappeared. On another occasion
he saw a white lady lying along the bridge at Newtownbutler who
suddenly vanished.

CASTLE ARCHDALE

Castle Archdale was once owned by the Archdale family, who
arrived during the Plantation of Ulster in 1614.

John Archdale built the castle in 1615 on a T-plan with a
surrounding defensive bawn. Rory Maguire destroyed it during
the 1641 Irish Rebellion. It was rebuilt and destroyed again during
the Williamite Wars in 1689. It was rebuilt during the eighteenth
century and during the Second World War it was occupied by
American troops, who treated the old place very badly. All
that remains is a derelict castle and a huge cobbled courtyard
surrounded by buildings that house tea rooms and an interesting
information centre describing the vital role played by the property
during the war.

Castle Archdale's role arose after the British Government
negotiated, with the Irish Free State, for a safe corridor that allowed
planes to pass from Fermanagh over Donegal on their way to the
Atlantic Ocean.

The castle and the nearby bay became a major base for flying boats. PBY Catalinas and Short Sunderlands flying out from the base provided protection for Atlantic shipping against attack by German U-boats.

It was a Catalina stationed at Castle Archdale that sighted the German battleship *Bismarck* on 26 May 1941. The Catalina was hit by anti-aircraft fire but managed to shadow the vessel. Its actions led to the navy being able to sink the *Bismarck* the following day.

Around 2,500 people were housed at Castle Archdale in its heyday.

The museum housed at Castle Archdale describing Fermanagh's war effort is well worth a visit. If you plan to visit it is as well to check beforehand to make sure it's open. The grounds are also worthwhile and there's no difficulty in visiting them.

Today there is a caravan site sitting on the concrete maintenance area where the aircraft were once serviced.

President Roosevelt is reported as having said: 'The Second World War could not have been won without the North of Ireland's war effort.' Fermanagh played a vital role.

CASTLE CALDWELL

Castle Caldwell is the former home of the Caldwell family who started Belleek Pottery (See Chapter 7). The castle is now a ruin. The grounds are a nature reserve with pleasant walks.

5

FERMANAGH FOLK TALES

This chapter begins with a few humorous tales because that is the type of story Fermanagh people enjoy most. I once asked the reason and my informant said: 'With our miserable wet climate and miserable history and what with the effects of the recent Troubles and all, we need something to keep our spirits up, so we do!'

THE CHAIRMAN

A local historical society wanted a particular man to come along and chair a panel of speakers.

One of the speakers was very pompous. He felt proud because he'd managed to get the person they wanted to act as chairman. They'd had to wait months, but eventually the great day had arrived and the speaker introduced their guest. 'Ladies and gentlemen,' he said, 'the ancient Greeks believed that sometimes a special child is born. When that happens one of the gods comes down to earth and kisses it. If he kisses it on the foot, the child becomes a great athlete. If he kisses it on the lips it is a great orator and if he kisses it on the hand it becomes a great artist and so on.

'Now, ladies and gentleman, I don't know where the gods kissed our chairman. All I can say is, he's a great chairman!'

THE DUNCE

In the past many teachers had no understanding of and no patience with children who were not academic. Such children were often picked on, stuck at the back of the room, continually scolded and made to wear a dunce's hat.

A teacher had a boy in his class who he thought was so stupid he told him to stay at home if he expected a visit from an inspector.

One day the teacher was horrified when he glanced out the window and saw the inspector arriving unexpectedly. The dunce was sent to the back of the class in the hope that his presence would go unnoticed.

The inspector was vain and the most sincere admirer of his appearance. He was wearing a fancy scarf and a long coat. He took his coat off and hung it carefully over the teacher's chair, folded his scarf neatly and placed it on a desk before taking his glasses off and polishing them. He opened his case, looked at the class and asked: 'Does anyone in here know my age?'

Nobody answered.

'Come on,' said the inspector, 'have a go! Guess.'

The dunce put his hand up and said, 'Please Sir, I think you're 42.'

'Aren't you the quare clever fella!' said the inspector. 'How did you work that out?'

'Well, my big brother's 21 and my mother's always telling him he's a half edjiot.'

THE MIRROR

There was once a man who lived in the bogs. It's difficult to make a living on such poor land but he worked hard, raised a large family and grew old.

The old man had never been fussy about his appearance and as he grew older he became even more untidy and careless. He spent all his time slapping about in a pair of muddy wellington boots and an old ragged coat.

How could I have let myself go?

One day his wife, Biddy, said: 'Why don't you take life a bit easier now? The children have left home. There's only the pair of us. Why don't you take a day off, go to the market and enjoy yourself.'

The old man thought that was a good idea and did as his wife suggested. When he got to the market he discovered things had greatly changed since the last time he'd been there. There were fewer animals and a much wider selection of goods. He spent some time looking at cows and goats then went and prowled round the stalls. He was intrigued by a stall selling bric-a-brac and picked up a small hand mirror. 'Lorny bless us!' he exclaimed. 'There's a picture of my father!' It was reasonably priced so he bought it.

On the way home the old man thought: 'I didn't buy anything for Biddy so I'll not let on that I bought a picture of my father for myself. I'll keep it hidden in my pocket. Biddy never did like him and there's no point in annoying her.

Every now and then, when he thought Biddy wasn't looking, he'd sneak the 'photo' out of his pocket and look at it.

Biddy noticed a change in her husband's behaviour. She often spied him taking something out of his pocket and stand looking at it and began to suspect he'd become interested in another woman.

One day, when the old man was sitting dozing by the fire, she slipped her hand into his pocket, lifted the mirror out and looked at it.

'I was right!' she muttered. 'He does fancy another woman. But look at the cut of her! I needn't bother about such an auld hairpin!' But, the situation worried her much more than she cared to admit. She kept waking up in the middle of the night, lying awake and wondering about the other woman. Who was she? Did her husband love her? What would she do if her old man decided to leave her? Eventually she decided to go and have a chat with the parish priest.

The priest had been there a long time and had become careless about his appearance. The parish was very remote, very poor and the priest was very old so the bishop had more or less forgotten about it.

Biddy told the priest her story and gave the mirror to him. The priest looked at it. 'Woman dear,' he said, 'I don't know what you're worrying about! You're raving. Sure that's the parish priest who was here before me.'

THE GOLDEN APPLES OF LOUGH ERNE

A long time ago Ireland was once ruled by a great king called Conn. He had a wonderful wife, Eda, who gave birth to a son. They named the baby Conn-eda, because he inherited all the gifts of each of his parents.

Unfortunately Queen Eda became ill and died. King Conn missed her terribly so the druids talked him into marrying again. At first his new wife seemed like Queen Eda. She was gentle, wise and fair in her judgements. She gave King Conn several more children and appeared happy and contented.

As time went by the new queen realised Conn-eda was his father's favourite and would eventually inherit the kingdom. She became very annoyed because she wanted her son to have it. She thought: 'If Conn-eda was dead my son would get everything. I wish I could kill Conn-eda, but I can't risk doing that in case I'm found out,' so she sought advice from an enchantress.

The enchantress said: 'Take this game of chess, challenge the prince to a game and suggest the winner should have the power to place the loser under a geasa. I'll make sure you win. When that happens tell the prince his geasa is either to go into exile or bring you, within the space of a year and a day, the three golden apples from the garden of the king of the Firbolg, along with his black steed and Samer, his supernatural hound.

'The king lives at the bottom of Lough Erne and if Conn-eda is foolish enough to try and bring you what you want he'll surely die!'

The queen was pleased, did as was suggested, won the game and said to Conn-eda: 'I put you under this geasa. Either go into exile or visit the garden under Lough Erne, which belongs to the king of the Firbolg, and bring me three of his golden apples, his black steed *(each dubh)* and his hound with supernatural powers *(coileen con na mbuadh)*. You must fulfil your geasa within one year and one day.'

Conn-eda decided he was definitely not going into exile. He would try to bring the queen the three golden apples, the black steed and the supernatural hound. He realised his decision meant facing great danger so went to the Great Druid, Fionn Dadhna, to ask for advice.

The Great Druid said: 'That's a terrible thing you've been asked to do. I think it's next to impossible … I'll need time to think about it … I'll have to use all my powers of sorcery to see if I can help … Come back and see me again tomorrow.'

Next day when Conn-eda returned and the Great Druid said, 'My dear son, that's an awful geasa. I think it's impossible. The queen has a bad heart. She hopes you will go to your death. Are you really sure you want to go ahead?'

'Yes!'

'Then be very careful. I suspect Ireland's greatest Druidess is the only person who would have suggested such a geasa. She's the King of Lough Erne's sister so that would make sense. Her powers are so great I'm afraid I can't be of much help.

'I suggest you go and talk to the bird with the human head. That bird knows everything about the past, the present and the future, but it's very difficult to find his hiding place. It's even more difficult to get a straight answer out of him but I think I can help you with him. Take my shaggy little steed and mount him immediately. He'll bring you to the bird, who'll become visible in three days' time. Take this precious jewel with you. Give it to the bird. It'll act as a sweetener and make him more likely to help.'

The prince thanked the Great Druid. He mounted the shaggy steed and the pair set off together to see if they could find the bird with the human head. At last the shaggy steed spotted it perching high up on a tree. Conn-eda held the jewel up to the bird and asked for advice.

The bird flew down, took the jewel, carried it up to the top of a high cliff, looked down and said in a loud, croaking human voice: 'I have decided to help you. There's a stone under your right foot. Lift it up. You'll find a ball of iron underneath. Lift it up, get back on your horse and throw the ball in front of you. If you allow your horse to follow it, it'll direct your footsteps.'

Conn-eda did as the bird suggested and the horse followed the rolling ball to the edge of Lough Erne, where it rolled into the water and became invisible.

The little horse turned round and said to Conn-eda, 'Take care! You're in great danger. Get down off my back and put your hand into my left ear. You'll find a small bottle of all-heal in a little wicker basket there. Take it out and look after it carefully because it'll help you survive. Once you've done that get up on to my back as quickly as possible.'

Conn-eda was astonished and gasped: 'I didn't know you could talk!'

The horse laughed and said: 'There's a lot you don't know! The Great Druid put me under a spell, but we haven't time to worry about that now. We've a job to do. Let's get on with it. Let's go together under the waters of Lough Erne.'

So Conn-eda and the little horse walked into Lough Erne and disappeared underneath its dark waters. They found a beautiful country at the bottom of the lough and its surface appeared like the sky above their heads.

The ball jumped along in front of them. They followed it until they came to a causeway leading to an island in the middle of a lake. It was guarded by three huge ugly serpents, who rose high in the air and hissed a loud warning.

'Now,' said the horse, 'open the little basket. You'll find three pieces of meat inside. Take them out. I'll gallop past the serpents while you hold tight on to my back and throw a piece of meat into each of the serpents' mouths as we pass them. Take careful aim because if you miss they'll swallow us alive!'

Conn-eda's aim was unerring.

'Bare benison and victory!' yelled the steed and celebrated by jumping high into the air before landing on to the island. 'You are a youth who deserves to prosper. Now tell me, are you all right?'

'Yes! I'm fine.'

'You're a prince who deserves to succeed,' said the steed. 'That's one danger past. We've only two more to face.'

The pair followed the ball until they came to a high mountain that was covered in flames.

'Hold on like grim death,' said the steed, 'I'll have to try and jump over that.'

Conn-eda crouched low over the horse's back as it sprang from the earth, soared like an arrow over the mountain and landed on the other side. They found themselves on a road outside the gate of what looked like a beautiful city.

'Are you still alive?' asked the horse.

'Yes, but only just! I'm in agony. I've been badly burnt.'

'You're still alive so I'm convinced you're a young man who's sure to meet supernatural success and benisons. Get off my back, open the little bottle and put some of the all-heal on your wounds.'

Conn-eda did as he was told and was instantly healed.

'Now,' said the horse, 'we're going to meet our final danger. You're going to find this difficult, but you must do it. It's very important.

'Look in my right ear. You'll find a small knife there. Take it out and cut my throat so I bleed to death, skin me, dress up in my hide and walk through the gate in the city's walls. Go straight to the palace and ask for an audience with the king.'

Conn-eda was very upset. He put his arms around the horse's neck and hugged him. 'I can't possibly do that,' he said. 'You've been a good friend. I've learnt to love you. I couldn't hurt you, never mind kill you.'

'Listen Conn-eda. You must do as I ask. If you don't we'll both die in agony. You've done everything I've told you so far. We've come safely through terrible danger together. You trusted me before. You must trust me now. Do as I ask as quickly as possible. The longer you delay the greater the danger.'

Conn-eda couldn't bear the idea of killing his friend.

'Come on!' urged the little horse. 'Trust me. Do as I say. Give me a quick, merciful death. I'd much rather have that than for us both to die in agony in a few minutes' time.'

Conn-eda realised he had no choice so reached into the little horse's right ear and found the penknife. He was blinded by tears as he stepped in front of the horse and pointed the knife at its throat. The dagger leapt out of his hand by some strange druidic power and sank itself into the horse's throat. In an instant the animal was dead. Conn-eda threw himself on the ground beside his steed and cried his heart out.

When he'd recovered he gave himself a mental shake and said aloud: 'I must make sure my dear friend didn't die in vain. I must do what he told me.' He made sure the animal was dead, flayed it, wrapped his skin around his body and walked through the gate leading to the city. He glanced back at his dear dead friend and saw a terrible sight. Bare bones, blood and guts lying in a heap.

There was a sudden flapping of wings and a crowd of vultures flew over and began pulling lumps of flesh off the corpse. Conn-eda couldn't bear it. He began yelling and waving his arms around as he ran towards his friend's body. He chased the vultures away, and on impulse took the tiny bottle of all-heal (íce) out of his pocket and poured it on the bloody corpse.

He watched in amazement as the heap of bones and blood began to bubble and boil. They took the shape of a handsome prince, who jumped up, hugged him and said: 'Conn-eda, thank you very much.

'The Druid, Fion Badhna is one wicked man. He put a spell on me that turned me into a shaggy little horse. He was forced to give me up when you came and asked him for help.

'My sister, Ireland's Greatest Druidess, told the wicked queen to put you under a geasa. She wanted to keep you safe, so decided to send you to our brother, the King of Lough Erne. I know he'll be delighted to see us and he'll give you the three golden apples, his black steed and his supernatural hound.'

When they arrived at the palace the King of Lough Erne made the prince and Conn-eda very welcome and said to Conn-eda: 'You've one year and one day to complete your task. Why don't the pair of you stay here and go home on the last day?

'I bet by that time the wicked queen'll be very pleased with herself. I bet she'll think she's got rid of you. I bet she'll be so annoyed to see you complete with three golden apples, my black steed and my supernatural hound she'll drop dead with disappointment.'

Conn-eda did as the king suggested and on the last day of his quest set out for home. When the guards saw him in the distance they told King Conn his son was on the horizon riding on a fine black steed with a huge hound running along beside him. The queen heard the news, ran up inside the tower and looked out over the battlements.

When she saw Conn-eda her heart was filled with horror. 'What'll happen to me now?' she wondered. 'The king'll know I tried to get rid of his favourite son. Will he throw me in the dungeon? Or have me beheaded? Or perhaps burnt at the stake? Oh the humiliation! I couldn't bear it.' With that she threw herself on to the ground below and was killed outright.

King Conn was delighted to have Conn-eda home again and said: 'I can see, my dear son, that you have reached manhood. I feel you should have a man's responsibilities so I'm going to give you a large piece of land to rule.'

The land given to Conn-eda was originally called Conn-eda. Over the course of time the name changed to Connaught.

MURTY MÓR AND MURTY BEAG

In days of old, when knights were bold and turkeys chewed tobacco there was a miller who loved children. Unfortunately he didn't have any of his own, but he had two sisters who had one son each. He grew to love the two lads and brought them into his business.

Murty Mór and Murty Beag

Both boys were called Murty, so to differentiate between the two, he added a descriptive term to their name. He called one Murty Mór (mór means big) and the other Murty Beag (beag means small).

Murty Mór was a big ignorant hallion, disliked by one and all. He was jealous of Murty Beag, who was what could only be described as a wee dote. Everyone loved him.

One night the two men were working on the rafters of the mill when Murty Beag slipped, fell to the ground below and was knocked unconscious.

Murty Mór was delighted. 'Now's my big chance,' he thought. 'I'll fix him!' He heated a poker red hot in the fire and used it to put Murty Beag's eyes out. 'Heh! Heh! Heh!,' he chuckled. 'Murty Beag'll be blind. You can't work if you can't see. He'll get the sack and the mill will be mine, all mine!'

Murty Beag regained consciousness in the middle of the night. He lay quietly on the floor, trying to work out where he was and feeling worried because his eyes were sore and he couldn't see. While he was lying quietly cats came into the mill and began talking to each other. One cat said: 'I heard the princess is very ill.'

A second cat replied, 'Yes, that's true and I think humans are stupid.'

'Why do you say that?'

'Because they'd let the princess die when there's an old well in the corner of the courtyard of this mill that cures all ills. She'd be better immediately if somebody had the sense to give her a drink of its waters.

'The king's so worried about his daughter he's promised half his kingdom to anyone who can cure her. I'm so sorry I'm just a cat and can't give her some of that magic water! Come on! It's time to get moving. We'd better find a few rats and mice for dinner.'

Murty Beag listened to the cats leaving the barn then crawled along the floor and felt for the door. When he found it he stood up, opened it, waited a few minutes to get his bearings and set off across the courtyard towards the well. He splashed his eyes with its healing waters and his sight returned. He filled a bottle full of the well's water and set out for the castle.

When Murty Beag reached the castle gate he told the guards he'd brought a cure for the princess. He was taken to the room where she lay, propped up in a beautiful bed. He held the bottle to her lips and she sipped the water. The colour returned to her cheeks and she sat up looking the picture of health. The king was delighted and gave Murty Beag all the gold, silver and precious stones he could carry.

When Murty Beag got back to the mill Murty Mór asked him what had happened. Murty Beag told him everything, all about the cats, the healing waters and the princess.

Murty Mór was very curious. He wanted to hear the cats talking. He could hardly wait for nightfall. He planned to hide under a pile of sacks. Sure enough, about midnight, the cats came into the barn and started talking. They were very annoyed. One cat said: 'Somebody must have been listening to us last night because the king's daughter's cured. She must have been given water out of the well.'

Another cat growled: 'I wonder if the listener's still here?' They searched the barn and found Murty Mór hiding under the sacks. They were furious and tore him to bits. There was nothing left but his boots and nobody ever knew what happened to him.

The princess she kept thinking and thinking about Murty Beag. She loved his smile and thought he was the nicest man she had ever met. She asked if she could see him again.

Murty Beag was delighted. The minute he'd seen the princess he'd fallen in love. He was a modest young man and thought the princess wouldn't want to be bothered with a commoner like him. After all, he was nothing but a poor miller and she was of royal blood. His heart was in his mouth when he was asked to go back to the palace to meet her again.

The young couple chatted for hours, decided they'd like to get married and asked the king for his consent. It was granted and they lived happy ever after.

IRELAND'S FIRST STORY OF ADULTERY AND JEALOUSY

Parthalán was the leader of the second group of people, called the Muintir Partholóin, who invaded Ireland about 300 years after

Noah's flood. The invaders found Ireland was an uninhabited island and began farming, cooking and building.

Parthalán and his wife, Delgnat, went to live on a small island at the head of the Erne's estuary. One day, when Parthálan was out hunting, Delgnat seduced a servant boy called Topa. After they had made love they drank some of Parthalán's special ale. The only way they could do that was to use a golden straw to sip it.

Parthalán was thirsty when he came back from hunting and lifted his ale to his mouth. He was furious and very jealous because he tasted the mouths of Delgnat and Topa on the golden straw. He flew into a rage, killed Topa and attempted to slaughter Delgnat. Her dog, Saimhir tried to protect her and ended up being killed.

Delgnat was furious and shouted at Parthálan: 'What happened was your own fault! You shouldn't have left me alone with Topa. You can't expect a woman to be able to resist honey when it is placed before her, or a cat to resist milk, or a child to resist meat. You're unreasonable expecting me to remain faithful. You went away and I didn't know if you'd come back or not!'

Parthalán must have felt remorse because he forgave Delgnat and the couple called their island Inis Samira, after her dog, Saimhir, who had died courageously trying to defend his mistress.

This story about Delgnat's lack of fidelity records how Inis Samira, the island on which she lived with her husband, got its name and it is Ireland's first story of adultery and jealousy.

LORD BENBOW'S TABLE

Benbow is a mountain that rises up steep and sharp above Manorhamilton, near the border between County Fermanagh and County Leitrim. It's a lovely wild land, full of small, unmarked roads leading back and forth over the border. It's very easy to get lost there.

There was a poor widower who lived above Manorhamilton, high up on the steep slopes of Benbow. He lived so high up the mountain that local people called him the Lord of Benbow.

The soil is poor and thin on Benbow so the poor widower found it impossible to earn a decent living. All he had on earth was a tiny, one-roomed shack to live in, a few goats, a cow and a son who was so lazy he wouldn't get out of bed in the morning.

The son was very handsome. All the local girls fancied him and thought they could teach him good habits if they could pin him down as a husband. The young man went out razzle dazzling every night. He'd a great time chasing women and next day he was so tired he couldn't get out of bed. He was useless.

The old man kept saying to his son: 'You're no good. You'll never amount to anything. You can't do a hand's turn. What are you going to do when I snuff it and you're left with the farm to run? Starve! That's what!'

The son paid no attention. All he'd say was: 'Some day I'll be rich.'

One day the son was so annoyed by his father continually asking him to work that he decided to leave home. He woke up early and took the cow to the market in Manorhamilton. It was a handsome beast because the old man made excellent poiteen and the cow was well fed on the waste. The son sold it for a good price and used the money to buy himself a grand suit of clothes, a cane, shoes and a watch and chain. He'd a great day swaggering up and down the town chatting to the girls. He'd even more 'come hither' with them now he was so well dressed he cut a great dash.

When the market was over and all the girls had gone home he decided to take the boat to England.

When he landed in England he walked along a road until he came to the grand entrance belonging to a nobleman's castle. He walked into the garden, plucked a rose and was fitting it to his buttonhole when a voice said: 'You're trespassing.'

He looked round and saw a lovely girl standing beside him. They'd a bit of craic during which he said: 'My father's Lord Benbow. He lives on Benbow Mountain in Ireland.'

The girl was impressed and said: 'You'll have to meet my father.'

She took the son into the castle and found the nobleman sprawling in a chair. The girl said: 'Father, I want to introduce you to Lord Benbow's son. He's just come over from Ireland.'

The nobleman looked at the son and said: 'Lord Benbow? I've never heard of him!' He took down a large book, went through it and said: 'There's no mention of Lord Benbow here.' He felt very suspicious but began talking to the son, who answered very nicely.

Lord Benbow? Never heard of him!

The nobleman was impressed and asked: 'Where are you staying tonight?' The son said: 'In the big hotel in the village. I passed it on the way here.'

'You can't possibly stay there. We've plenty of room in the castle. You must stay here. I know my daughter'll enjoy having company of her own age.'

The son did enjoy staying in the castle. He felt he'd been born for that type of life and he and the girl were all over each other.

The nobleman was still suspicious and warned his daughter by saying: 'Don't get too great with that fellow. We don't know anything about him.'

The girl said: 'I love him and I'm going to marry him.'

Her father begged her to be sensible and not get married until he sent a servant to Ireland to find out more about Lord Benbow.

The servant reached Manorhamilton late one afternoon and asked local people where Lord Benbow lived. They said: 'Do you see thon wee cabin near the top of the mountain? That's where he lives.' The servant asked for directions and the locals pointed at a pad road and said, 'That goes most of the way up.'

It was a beautiful evening and nowhere is more beautiful than Fermanagh when the sun is shining. The servant was charmed by the scenery. When he got to the cabin the goats were butting each other. The old man had pulled aside his shalfoskee (in this case it was a straw mat he put across the entrance of the cabin to keep the wind out). He could be seen sitting on a stool eating from a tin of stirabout, which he was supporting on his knees. He had a ponger (a word used in south-west Ulster for a tin mug) beside him. He bade the stranger welcome, gave him share of his meal and his own bed.

When the servant took his leave next day he thought the old man appeared depressed and asked: 'Is there something bothering you?'

'Yes,' he said, 'I think maybe I was too hard on my son. He upped and left me. I don't know if he's dead or alive.'

The servant said: 'He's alive and well and going to be married,' and the old man cheered up.

The servant went back to his master in England and told the nobleman: 'I got to Lord Benbow's residence and heard the clank of armour. The guard was out because it was sunset. I went in and found old Lord Benbow having a meal, which he shared with me. All your wealth couldn't buy what we supped off. You never ate food like it in the whole of your puff! And a thousand pounds wouldn't buy the wick of the lamp that lit that room! It was unbelievable!'

The nobleman felt content with his servant's report. The young couple were allowed to marry and were very happy.

Now, I'm going to tell you what traditional Irish storytellers used to say when they'd finished telling a tale: 'That was every word of the truth I was telling ye, and not one word of a lie, and, if it was a lie, I didn't make it up!'

THE COONEEN GHOST

Mrs Murphy and her family, husband Michael, her son James and her five daughters, Anne, Mary, Bridget, Catherine and Jane-Anne, moved into an isolated farmhouse in Cooneen in the year 1913.

Shortly after they moved her husband fell out of his cart and was killed. A few nights later the youngest daughters were in bed and James was out visiting a neighbour as Mrs Murphy and Anne sat quietly chatting beside a turf fire. Suddenly they heard the children scream. The walls were thumped and heavy footsteps rang throughout the building. They didn't pay much attention. They thought somebody was playing tricks, but it was the beginning of a nightmare. They frequently heard banging noises on walls, doors knocking and the sound of heavy footsteps, yet nobody was there. Then it became even more unpleasant. Ghostly shadows appeared and disappeared on walls, cups and saucers flew off the dresser and smashed themselves on the floor, beds were lifted in the air, bedclothes were snatched off sleeping children and a cold evil presence pervaded the house.

Neighbours came to stay with the family and experienced the ghost's activity, as did the local priests. The ghost could whistle, make a sound like a kicking horse and hiss like a snake. It replied to questions by tapping out answers and could tap out tunes such as 'Boyne Water' and 'The Soldier's Song'.

Mrs Murphy moved the children's bedroom to the end of the house but the ghost followed them.

Father Coyle, a young curate from Maguiresbridge, was given permission to perform two exorcisms. They didn't work. The ghost appeared to be amused by them and continued torturing the family.

The Murphys were terrified. They had pinned their hopes on Father Coyle getting rid of the ghost and he'd failed. To make matters worse the neighbours began to ostracise them. Rumours were rife. It was said that James Murphy had developed an

The way yon ghost tortured the Murphys was terrible.

interest in the occult and the Murphys had brought the trouble on themselves. They found the rumours terribly upsetting and decided the best thing they could do was emigrate to America.

The family were delighted as they left Fermanagh and boarded a ship bound for New York. They thought they'd left the ghost behind, but that was not to be. It came with them! It kicked up such a noise around their cabin that other passengers complained to the captain. He didn't believe in ghosts and threatened to put them off the ship if they didn't stop making such a terrible din!

When they reached New York they were forced to move house five times before the ghost finally left them in peace.

Ghosts usually can't cross water and if they do manage to do so the time they can stay away from their place of origin is limited. Recently there's been a rumour saying the ghost has returned to the old cottage in Cooneen. It is now an abandoned, derelict building with a dank evil atmosphere. It is not a place to be visited alone, especially after dark!

6

CONDITIONS BEFORE AND AFTER THE GREAT FAMINE

'Rattle my bones over the stones
I'm a poor pauper who nobody owns'
(An old saying from the days of the workhouses)

After partition of Ireland in 1922 the government of the then Free State of Ireland collected stories about the Great Famine from old people who could remember it, or had been told about it by elderly relatives. The Government of Northern Ireland did not do that. This neglect of local history caused a false perception, namely that Northern Ireland was not affected. That is entirely untrue, County Fermanagh, along with the rest of Ulster, was devastated. The only places that escaped were small isolated pockets in remote places such as islands. John Reihill says Iniscormkish Island, the island on which he and his ancestors lived, was not affected.

HOUSING

Sod Houses

The census of 1842 showed that nearly half of the rural population lived in sod houses. They were, as the name suggests, built from sods of earth stacked on top of each other and thatched with any material that happened to be handy, such as heather, whins, marron grass, straw and so on. They had no windows and the door was formed by leaving a space in the walls for an entrance.

Sod houses were damp and drafty. William Carleton, the author who lived on the border between County Tyrone and County Fermanagh, described how green willow branches were tied together to form an 'old man' (corrag), approximately 6ft (2m) in height. It was put on the windy side of the door to cut the draft. It was dark inside a sod house and even darker with the corrag in place!

Sod houses soaked up moisture in Ireland's damp climate and began to crumble within ten years. Desperate attempts were made to prop them up with branches of trees and so on. A strong wind could cause them to collapse and kill their occupants.

The death rate during the Great Famine has been underestimated as a sod house is almost invisible because it merges into its background. Its starving, diseased occupants crawled into the miserable place they thought of as home, it collapsed round them and they died as they had lived – uncounted.

People living in sod houses were lucky compared to thousands of homeless people, who lived in bog holes thatched with branches. Other individuals occupied caves or dug holes in banks. They, like the occupants of many sod houses, went uncounted, so the 1842 census is inaccurate.

Grinding poverty caused the poor to be dressed in rags that didn't even cover their bodies in a modest fashion. Whole families, parents, grandparents and six, seven or more children lived in squalor, along with the family pig, in a single room, which could have been in a sod house.

Housing for Comparatively Prosperous Farmers

Comparatively more prosperous farmers lived in a simple cottage built from stones designed in a straight line with one room opening out of another. The outer door was often a half door, that is one that was divided into two so the lower half could be closed, to keep hens out, while the top was open allowing fresh air and light in.

Sometimes an L-shaped wall, called a jam wall, was built inside the outer door to keep the wind from blowing straight in. A small window was often placed in it so old granny, sitting by the fire, could see who was coming.

If the family became prosperous the house would have been 'raised', that is an upper storey was built on top of the ground floor.

When cottages were replaced their owners usually left them standing because of the belief that the old people, that is the people who once lived there, reappeared at night once everyone had gone asleep, to sit around the fire and have a bit of craic. They thought if the old house was removed these old spirits would be lost and haunt the family! There are still a few people living in County Fermanagh who find excuses not to remove stones from old houses. They are allowed to become derelict.

Housing the Wealthy

Wealthy people lived in large good-quality houses with fireplaces in every room and servants to attend their every need.

CAUSES OF THE GREAT FAMINE

The Potato and Farming Practices

It has been said that the humble potato caused the Great Famine (1845–47) that devastated Ireland's population. That is an exaggeration but there is an element of truth in it.

Sir Walter Raleigh (1552–1618), brought potatoes from America to Ireland and planted them at his Irish estate at Myrtle Grove, Youghal, near Cork. At first the potato was used as a delicacy in the large Anglo–Irish houses but it is easy to grow and quickly spread to the native population throughout Ireland.

Potatoes contain a lot of vitamin E, which helps to increase fertility, so the native population grew rapidly. Parents sub-divided their farms between their children. Every inch of land became cultivated, even poor marginal land along the fringes of sandy shores and on the tops of mountains. Today the outlines of potato beds may still be found in remote places such as on top of the Culiagh Mountains in County Fermanagh.

The population increase caused the land to become very overcrowded. Ulster had the highest percentage of small farms in the whole of Ireland, that is farms of 5 acres or less. High rents combined with high population density resulted in subsistence farming. People lived on a diet of potatoes. Monocultures are susceptible to disease and unfortunately the most common type of potato grown was the lumper. It has little, if any resistance to potato blight.

A family of six could live off 2 acres of land, provided they had a cow. The farm was divided into three sections. Potatoes were grown on one section, oats on another and the third section was used to grow grass. During the summer months the cow ate the grass while the family ate oats and potatoes. They found the month of June difficult because by that time the previous year's crop was exhausted and the next crop wasn't ready, so June became known as the 'hungry month'.

During the winter the cow fed on oats while the family continued to eat potatoes and oats.

The cow was important to the household's wellbeing because its waste fertilised the land. Manure was so precious it was stored in a heap outside the cottage door to keep it from being stolen and the family added their excrement! (This was in the days before anyone knew anything about the germ theory of disease so other parts of the world had similar practices.)

The humble pig was very important to the rural economy because its offspring were sold to pay the rent. That's why the pig was called 'the gentleman who pays the rent'.

The 1842 census showed people living in the parish of Tullahobagly in County Donegal (one of the counties adjacent to Fermanagh) owned 10 beds, 95 chairs and 243 stools between them. The vast majority of the population (9,000) slept on bags filled with straw. There is no reason to think the situation differed substantially from that found in Fermanagh's parishes.

Victorian Attitudes to Misfortune

Victorians believed that if you suffered from misfortune you must have done something very bad and were being punished by God. That belief was so strong that when Queen Victoria gave birth to a disabled baby, Prince John, he was kept hidden. It would never have done for her subjects to think she had annoyed the Almighty. It was difficult for anyone to believe it was right to help the starving Irish. It was their own fault they were dying of starvation. They must have annoyed God by being bad, lazy, feckless people and so on. And if somebody had annoyed the Almighty was it right to interfere with his punishment? As a result, the government's response was slow and the attitude of the general public was unsympathetic. No consideration was given to the extortionate rents they had to pay and the fact that ten ships of food were taken out of the country and sent to England for every one sent to bring help during the height of the famine. There wouldn't have been a famine if the Irish had been able to retain their own crops and hadn't been forced to use them to pay rent to avoid eviction.

Victorian attitudes to misfortune were shocking!

Water Supply

Cleanliness and good hygiene is impossible without a good, safe water supply, which was not available until towards the end of the nineteenth century. As a result the poor became filthy and covered in lice. The well-off tended to keep their distance because of the strong possibility of catching lice and the unpleasant stench of body odour. Hence, the wealthy didn't realise how serious was the situation.

As the population grew, pressure on land became greater and greater and the amount of waste produced increased. It sank into the water table beneath the soil and seeped into rivers, streams and wells. Sewage ran down the streets of towns in a disgusting stream and ended up in the water supply. Horses were used for transport. They added urine as well as dung to the general filth, as did animals travelling from one place to another and at local fairs. Liquid from their excrement also sank through soil and ended up in the water supply. Contaminated water reached wells and water pumps and caused death from waterborne diseases such as typhoid. There was no alternative to either using disease-laden water from local wells and streams or from the neighbourhood pump.

Some very wealthy households had proper flushing toilets, although most used large china 'potties', something like the ones used to toilet-train babies today, but richly ornamented and much bigger. Although that was more pleasant for the owner than using a manure heap there was no satisfactory place to empty it. It must have been a nasty job for the poor servant who was expected to get rid of the contents.

The 'proper' toilets were pleasant to use but contained hidden dangers. There was no proper sewage disposal system and waste had to go somewhere. Some people stored it in their basements, then pumped it out on to the streets at night, where it ran in a filthy stinking stream into the water supply, joining the effluent from the rest of the population. On 23 December 1846 the following letter, describing another problem, appeared in the local newspaper, the *Impartial Reporter*:

Sir,

I have just heard that it is intended to make a graveyard on the grounds at the poorhouse. Was there ever such a project? A place for burial in such a place!

All under the poorhouse ground is limestone rock, through which water finds its way as rapidly as down a river course. Granted! Then bury hundreds of putrified bodies, the fluid putrescence will flow into cisterns at the pumps, and what comforting reflections must occupy the minds of those who use such water.

Tea made out of stewed old hag, and the master's whiskey punch diluted with the essence of a boiled beggar man would be rare novelties.

> Disgusting,
> Sir
> yours etc.
> An engineer

The situation didn't improve until Queen Victoria's husband, Prince Albert, died from typhoid, caused by contaminated water in Windsor Castle. His death motivated the government to take action and begin work on providing a safe water supply.

Contaminated water and resulting disease played a significant part in the death rate caused by the Great Famine because bodies weakened by hunger have a lowered resistance to disease.

Food, Diet and Cooking Methods

The majority of the population had nothing to eat apart from potatoes, washed down with buttermilk.

Potatoes and buttermilk constitute a good diet except it is lacking in vitamin A, which is essential for good sight. As a result people, if they lived to be old, became blind. That didn't happen if they could grow, and keep, carrots, which are a good source of vitamin A.

Potatoes were never wasted. Children took cold potatoes to school for lunch, fishermen took some with them when they went fishing. Leftovers were mixed with flour, a little milk and some butter, made into a dough, rolled flat and baked on a griddle to make potato bread. (Today potato bread may be bought in supermarkets and home bakeries, or supplied by restaurants and hotels as part of the famous Ulster fry.) Anything left over was fed to animals and whole potatoes were pushed into the fire to feed hungry strangers.

'Kitchen' was the term used to describe anything taken with potatoes. That could be a dish of salty water into which the family dipped their potatoes before eating them.

Local author William Carleton, who lived during the Great Famine, described a way of attempting to add taste to potatoes called potatoes and point. A small piece of salted herring or bacon was hung on the chimney breast. Before eating a potato each member of the family pointed it at the chimney breast. The flavour of the herring or bacon was said to be transferred to the potato, but then imagination is a wonderful thing.

Carleton also described potato and egg milk. Some water was boiled over a fire and eggs were beaten into it. The resultant 'egg milk' was passed around the family so each member could dip a potato into it. It was a handy way of sharing a few eggs among a large family. Families of seventeen were not unusual. A large family was thought to be an insurance against destitution in old age as offspring were expected to look after aged parents and run the farm.

Women cooked over an open fire. The fire was placed in the middle of sod houses. Some of the ensuing smoke went out through the hole in the roof above the fire, the rest swirled around inside, causing eye irritation. As a result women's eyes became raw and red and they frequently developed eye cancers.

Stone-built houses had proper fireplaces, with chimneys, so the woman of the house was able to use a crook and crane to cook over an open fire. Normally the crane was attached to the left of the chimney breast so a right-handed woman could swing it back and forward using her left hand while her right hand was free to do finer jobs such as stirring the stew. If a woman was left-handed the crook was placed on the right side of the fire.

It was possible to tell how wealthy a house was by the number of cooking pots sitting on the hearth around the fireplace. The fewer the cooking pots, the poorer the family. Poverty-stricken families would have had one leaking old pot.

Wealthy people were able to afford a balanced diet with meat and plenty of fruit and vegetables.

The Famine Begins – 1845

The Great Famine began in the autumn of 1845. James Brown, who lived in Donaghnore, County Tyrone, said the first potato blight arrived on his farm in October 1845. In one night his potatoes

Would somebody help us!?

were struck with the disease, which blackened both the tops and the roots. Luckily the damage was only partial because the crop was almost mature before being struck. It was possible to use some potatoes for normal consumption and the rest were fed to pigs or made into starch.

Tyrone is adjacent to Fermanagh so the two counties must have had similar experiences. James Brown wrote notes about the famine that are stored in the Public Record Office in Belfast.

Desperate attempts were made to stop the blight spreading. They were useless due to the lack of scientific knowledge at the time. On Tuesday morning, 11 November 1845, the *Belfast Newsletter* had an article suggesting bog water could be used as an antiseptic to control the disease. Potato blight is caused by a fungus (Phytophthora infestans) that thrives in damp conditions so the suggested 'cure' was worse than useless.

Some landlords and their agents did their best to help their tenants, others used the inability to pay rent as an excuse to bully and harass them or clear the land. This led to civil unrest. The above newspaper contains a report from County Fermanagh about an attempt on the life of Follow Barton, a landlord who was 'lying in a very precarious state with two slugs which are supposed to be lodged in his lungs'. The reporter wrote: 'Crimes of this sort are not so much crimes of the individual as crimes of the whole community,' which was a Victorian reflection on morality of the day.

The Famine During 1846

On 3 August 1846 James and his sister Bella drove through County Fermanagh on their way to Bundoran. They were delighted to see fine potato crops thriving in the fields. They spent three days in Bundoran before returning home. During that short time the crops had become blackened, stinking and useless. It was a terrible disaster because the population had spent all its reserves surviving during the previous year.

During 1846 Indian corn and meal were brought from America for the first time. Food was in short supply and it became just as expensive as flour, so starving people ate anything they could find, nettles, charlock (wild mustard), blackberries, chickweed and so on.

Nettles were used as food in Scotland and the North-west of England as well as in Ireland. They grow higher and better in graveyards than anywhere else and people travelled miles to collect them. They are sometimes called kale, which is very confusing because inquests were sometimes carried out on those who had died of starvation. The coroner often reported a victim had nothing but kale in his or her stomach. Did he mean cabbage or nettles?

Nettles were also called 'nenaid' or in early modern Irish 'nentog', later spelt 'neanntog'. Nettles are a good food because they contain vitamin C and zinc. Vitamin C helps disease resistance while the zinc makes the effect stronger. They are also full of iron, which prevents anaemia.

Charlock belongs to the cabbage family. It has bright yellow flowers and grows to a height of between 1–2ft (30 and 50cm).

During the Great Famine many families lived on a few pence of meal each week. They boiled it with charlock to turn it into a soup and make it go further. Charlock causes stomach upsets and turns the skin of those eating it yellow. It's not the kind of thing anyone could have wanted to eat, as shown by the following account written by Samuel Burdy in *The Life of the Late Rev Philip Skelton* published in Dublin in 1792.

The Rev Philip Skelton went to Pettigo in 1757, almost 100 years before the Great Famine. (There were many periods of famine, but the Great Famine in Ireland was the one that had the most profound effect.) He visited a miserable cabin in Pettigo and was made very welcome by its owners. They had boiled some charlock, added a little salt and were eating it for breakfast. He was given a share and found the taste 'nauseous'. He went home, gathered charlock and ate it for breakfast on the following two days, after which his stomach turned against it and he felt really sorry for poverty-stricken people.

Newspaper Comments About the Great Famine

Many of the paupers left rural areas and went to the city in the hope of finding work. The *Belfast Newsletter* of 23 December 1845 stated: 'There are multitudes of paupers for every rich man to be counted in the crowds of a city or in the more scattered population of the country' and 'poverty is in itself a fertile mother of disease'.

Not everybody believed there really was a famine. The author of an article printed in the *Belfast Newsletter* of 10 February 1846 claimed that the reports of famine exaggerated the plight of the poor for political reasons, namely to 'give colour for the agitation of free trade'. He continued by quoting from *The Times*: 'All parties must unite, government, landlords, farmers and merchants, if need be, to avert the calamity, which we hope at present is exaggerated only for the purpose of serving a political party.'

During the spring and early summer of 1846 the potato crop looked healthy until the blight struck again in the middle of summer. On Tuesday, 8 September 1846 the *Belfast Newsletter* reported: 'Distress in almost all parts of Ireland is becoming so apparent, so stark, that all classes are determined to shut their eyes no longer.'

The *Belfast Newsletter* of Friday, 18 September 1846 told how increasing hardship was leading to disturbances. A large crowd gathered in Newtownbutler and said, if necessary, they would use force to obtain relief. They were pacified and dispersed quietly when the Earl of Erne promised to help. On the same day the British Association stated, 'the state cannot accede to these extravagant demands', while the *London Standard* reminded 'the English people' had helped people in Lisbon 100 years earlier who had been left destitute by an earthquake. It followed that it was unreasonable to maintain the famine had nothing to do with Britain.

Workhouses

Just before the Great Famine, the government decided to help the poor by building workhouses. The vast majority of workhouses, including those in County Fermanagh, were built to George Wilkinson's plan, an architect employed by the Irish Poor Law Commissioners.

In County Fermanagh workhouses were available for paupers in the following places: Enniskillen, Irvinestown or Lowtherstown, Roslea and Lisnaskea.

Lisnaskea workhouse differed from the others in that it had had a porter's lodge to one side of the administrative block, which was later used as a dispensary.

Workhouses were very impressive buildings. Poor starving people leaving a sod house, covered in lice and wearing ragged clothes must have felt intimidated being forced to approach the exterior of

We'll have to go to the workhouse

a building resembling a stately home. Notwithstanding their outer appearance, workhouses were harsh institutions.

On arrival you were stripped naked, your hair was hacked off and you were given a good scrub with carbolic soap in a bath containing Jeyes Fluid. After all that you were dressed in ugly workhouse clothes, which probably didn't fit, with shoes that were either too small or too big. You slept in a dormitory on a straw-filled tick mattress on a wooden platform.

Families were separated from each other. The women were housed with other women, men were housed with men, boys with boys and girls with girls. You never saw your family again. And you had to work hard. The men were employed splitting rocks. Women were given large quantities of oakum (old ropes impregnated with tar) to sort out. It was rough, unpleasant, dirty work. The idea was to remove the tar with a spike and separate it from the rope fibres. Sometimes women were asked to split stones, anything to keep them busy. It didn't matter how unpleasant or soul-destroying the task was as long as it gave the workhouse a bad reputation so people wouldn't want to go there.

Food in workhouses was awful but it was better than starving to death outside. Lisnaskea workhouse was similar to others. Meat was hardly ever eaten. Potatoes formed the staple diet. When potatoes were scarce they were weighed then boiled in nets to make sure every inmate got a fair, if small, share. When potatoes became unobtainable Indian meal was brought in. It was difficult to cook and spat and bubbled, causing people to say, 'You have to boil the devil out of it'. The inmates of Lisnaskea couldn't get used to it so the master asked for rice to be supplied instead. Cooking it was easier.

The old workhouses existed up until 1947, when they were abolished in the United Kingdom when the National Health Service came into being.

The late Angela Dillon was President of Banbridge Historical Society. Angela's Granny Bell was born in the late nineteenth century. She caught scarlet fever when she was a child and was taken to the fever hospital associated with Banbridge workhouse. She told Angela of her experiences in the hospital. Banbridge is in County Down but what happened there would have been similar in County Fermanagh.

Granny Bell said patients with diphtheria were separated from those with scarlet fever. She said people suffering from diphtheria had a very high temperature and an excruciatingly sore throat that became so swollen it cut off the air pipe leading to the lungs. When that happened the patient couldn't breathe and usually died.

Modern medicine has mostly eradicated diseases such as diphtheria and scarlet fever that were killers in the past. Granny Bell said children were housed on the same wards as the elderly. She didn't like them because they were cross and told the children to leave them alone and go away.

Granny Bell said when you were recovering from scarlet fever you were allowed out to play in the fresh air. The children used to stand and goggle as tiny coffins were carried across from the wards to the morgue, but they didn't think anything of it.

The old workhouses and fever hospitals brought back so many unhappy memories most of them were knocked down. Lisnaskea's workhouse has survived and at present a local committee is raising money to renovate it.

Enniskillen workhouse opened on 1 December 1845 and sixty-nine paupers were admitted. As time passed the effects of the famine increased and death stalked the land. The workhouses became more and more overcrowded. Increasing numbers of people died of fever because as the famine worsened so did the conditions. In Enniskillen workhouse in May 1847 there was an average of five deaths a day. Conditions became even worse, with fifty dying during the week of 3 June 1847. The cost of coffins was £10–£12 per week, so it was decided to bury the dead without coffins. A report in the *Impartial Reporter* on 10 June condemned the burials as follows:

> Will some one interested in the management of our poor house see that the dead paupers are buried out of sight, and beyond the reach of smell. When the wind blows North Easterly the effluvia reaches Enniskillen. When we noticed the slovenly burial of the poor on previous occasion, attention was paid for some time: but now it is worse than ever. Earth and lime should be spread over the ground, and the bodies buried deeper in future.

Bodies of victims of the Great Famine who died in Enniskillen workhouse were found by workmen building the car park for the new Erne Hospital. They were removed and buried properly with all due respect. Such bodies must be treated with care, not only because they are human remains but because it is still possible to become infected with cholera, which can survive in soil for a very long time.

What happened in Enniskillen workhouse happened throughout Ireland. So many people died it was impossible to give everyone a proper burial. Ireland is still dotted with famine mounds and many have been destroyed by becoming buried under new developments such as roads and car parks.

While many people did their best to help paupers during the Great Famine others, such as absentee landlords, merchants and some individuals employed in the workhouses, exploited the situation to line their own pockets. Enniskillen workhouse was instructed by the board of guardians to buy quantities of tea and sugar. When they paid a visit to the workhouse in March 1847 they discovered workhouse officials had retained and sold it for their own benefit. In Roslea, famine relief was distributed from Mr Chamber's yard in the form of Indian meal porridge. Once it was boiled and allowed to cool, a watery liquid called 'shirings' came to the top of the porridge. It had little nutritional value and was given to the paupers while the solid porridge was fed to Chamber's pigs.

FAMINE RELIEF

Road Works

Eventually the government made a half-hearted attempt at famine relief by providing funds for road building. Unfortunately, starving people need to be paid promptly for work done and the organisation of the scheme was so poor that did not happen. As a result emancipated skeletons struggled to work, worked all day on empty stomachs and were not paid for months afterwards, by which time the poor souls had died of starvation. Another disadvantage was the number of useless roads built. They didn't go anywhere and could end in remote places such as the middle of bogs. Most of the original roads in Ireland were built to bend around the landscape to avoid bogs or places where flooding was likely. Folklore says that famine roads are straight so it is still possible to identify them today.

The Society of Friends

The work of Members of the Society of Friends, also called Quakers, was outstanding. They had a different attitude to the majority of Victorians; they believed that God was present in everyone and those who were suffering should be helped. They saw and understood the seriousness of the situation.

Quakers had several advantages denied the government that helped their efforts in famine relief. They had a well-developed system of committees and strong family connections, which kept them in close contact. Many Irish Quakers were merchants with experience of buying goods and moving them efficiently around the country. These skills were invaluable in an era of poor roads and a practically non-existent railway system.

They set up a committee in London to raise funds with a major Irish committee, based in Dublin, to look after grants of food and clothing. Many English Quakers came to Ireland to see the situation for themselves and to work on the ground.

The actions of Quakers were limited because they were few in number so they co-operated with, and helped, non-Quakers already operating relief schemes and became involved in collecting and distributing clothing. Most of the donated clothing came from England during the winter of 1846–7. The mainly female English committees either made clothes themselves or put pressure on

Many people emigrated

factories to donate them. During the following winter most of the clothing donations came from America, usually in the form of cloth, enabling the employment of people to turn it into clothes.

During 1847 Quakers changed the direction of the help they were giving because the government began to set up soup kitchens. The Quakers kept the system going until government structures were in place to take over. After that they helped to carry out a survey, which found the number of destitute people was so great it was well beyond their resources. They decided the best thing they could do was to help those who were not entitled to government aid. As a result they set up employment schemes so that people would have an income to enable them to support themselves.

Actions by Individuals

As the famine progressed local newspapers began to carry reports of functions organised in attempts to help the starving. Many landlords reduced rents, individuals did charitable deeds and many private individuals attempted to help the starving. There are many examples of that on record, for example, Lord Erne reduced the rents paid by his tenants.

A letter in the Public Record Office, written to the editor of the *Fermanagh Reporter* on 5 April 1878 by M. McCauley, who emigrated to Chicago in 1848, says he couldn't forget the time between 1846 and 1847 'when gaunt death and hunger stalked abroad and the wolf of hunger was at every poor man's door', when Christopher Nixon stood by the roadside near his home asking almost every passer-by if he, or she, was hungry. He then sent hungry people up to his house for a meal.

The *Impartial Reporter* of Friday, 2 October 1846 carried an address by the Earl of Erne to his tenants:

> Well my friends, I think we must agree upon this one thing, that the potato as a crop and as a food for the country is gone, at least for many years and I fear that in most places there will be no seed to be had. You know I have often told you that the cultivation of potatoes on too large a scale was very injurious to you by preventing your attention to other crops. It has been your custom to give all the manure to the potato crop and to neglect the rest of your farm … I will say no more in dispraise of a fallen enemy;

and I hope that you will one and all determine to become good farmers.

The Lace Industry

The Countess of Erne started a lace school in Lisnaskea in an attempt to provide work for starving tenants.

Mrs McClean, the wife of the Primate of the Church of Ireland, had an interest in lace making she passed on to her daughters, Lizzie, Sarah and Emily.

Her daughter, Emily, married the Reverend Tottenham, the rector at Inishmacsaint Church of Ireland. She organised lace-making classes in Benmore Rectory, with help from her sisters. These classes proved so popular they eventually moved to a larger premises in a disused dispensary in Derrygonnelly. Inishmacsaint lace is made entirely by hand using fine linen thread so it is very labour intensive.

Alan Cole, from the Science and Art Department, South Kensington Museum, London, and James Brennan, Principal of the Metropolitan School of Art in Dublin, toured Irish lace centres during the 1880s. They were very impressed by Ellen Hansard, in Inishmacsaint Lace School and gave her a bursary to attend Dublin Metropolitan School of Art. She enjoyed the course and returned to Inishmacsaint, eventually becoming principal lace teacher at the school. She was an excellent manager and Inishmacsaint lace became famous after it was exhibited at the Chicago World's Fair in 1892 and Queen Alexandra, Edward VII's wife, wore a yoke of Inishmacsaint lace at her coronation in 1902.

Because handmade lace is so labour intensive, so it is expensive. When lace-making machines were invented they destroyed the lace-making industry in Fermanagh.

The Lace Museum at Bellanaleck has a marvellous display of handmade lace, including some from Inishmacsaint.

THE FAMINE ENDS

The potato harvest improved in 1847 and the government said the Great Famine was over, but the effects lingered a long time. Seed potatoes were in short supply and emigration and the effects of starvation were felt for many years to come, so some maintain the Great Famine lasted from 1845 to 1851. So many people died, or emigrated, manual labourers were in short supply. It became cheaper to use machines and employ people to use them, a fact that encouraged the process of industrialisation.

In Fermanagh the time after the Great Famine was called 'the great silence' because the normal sounds of country life had ceased due to the high death rate and the vast number of people who emigrated.

7

THE GARDEN OF CELTIC SAINTS, BELLEEK POTTERY AND THE GEOPARK

THE GARDEN OF CELTIC SAINTS

The Garden of Celtic Saints is in the grounds of the Secret Heart church, Lisnarick Road, Irvinestown. It is more than a simple tourist attraction. The original concept was to provide a deeper experience than simple enjoyment, although it certainly is enjoyable.

The garden is essentially a sculpture garden with the sculptures protected from the elements by a series of 'houses'. They were carved out of wood by Jonas Raiskas, an artist who is a native of Lithuania. He came to Irvinestown in 2007, commissioned by Devonish Parish to carve the statues from native Irish oak. He worked from 2007–11.

The garden sets out to be a place of beauty and hope, prayer and reflection. One visitor, who lives in Irvinestown, said: 'My husband died last year. I was in a terrible state. I don't know what drew me up here but when I arrived I felt a great sense of peace. I felt he was near. Now I come and just wander around every day. I mightn't have time to spare but even a short visit helps me focus on the day and it's such a comfort.'

An Old Irish Blessing
May the road rise up to meet you.
May the wind always be at your back.
May the sun shine warm upon your face,
and the rains fall soft upon your fields.
  And until we meet again,
  May God hold you in the palm of His Hand.

BELLEEK POTTERY

Belleek Pottery was the brainchild of the local landlord, John Caldwell Bloomfield, who owned Castle Caldwell during the mid-nineteenth century. During the Great Famine he realised that many of his tenants were starving and wondered how he could enable them to earn an income through gainful employment.

Lord Caldwell was an amateur geologist. He began by ordering a geological survey of his land to see if he could find anything useful. He found that his property contained the type of clay suitable for making pots so he decided to build a pottery.

He had two friends, David McBirney, a successful Dublin businessman and the London architect, Robert William Armstrong, who became interested in his project. David McBirney helped finance the venture while Robert Armstrong designed, built and managed the pottery.

They began by making ordinary domestic products, however Robert Armstrong realised, to his great delight, that the local clay was special and could be used to produce a very thin, strong iridescent porcelain called Parian porcelain. Parian porcelain made the pottery famous. Manufacture began in 1863 and the factory opened its doors a year later. It was an instant success. Victorian ladies enjoyed showing guests the delicate shine on its surface and holding it up to the light to see the light shining through it. Queen Victoria loved it, as did the Prince of Wales. By 1865 the pottery was booming and supplying goods to India, Australia and America as well as to the nobility throughout the world.

Robert Armstrong and David McBirney had what was in those days a common sort of agreement, sealed by friendship and a gentleman's handshake; they didn't bother with any paperwork. As a result their agreement was not legally binding. When McBirney died in 1882 his heirs did not honour it and sacked Armstrong. He had spent his life building up the business and was heartbroken. He took the heirs to court, lost his case and died of a broken heart. His gentle ghost has been seen walking around the upper floors of the pottery he loved so dearly and, as for the heirs, they got their comeuppance. They were greedy and knew it would be easier and less expensive to produce ordinary pottery rather than the fine Parian porcelain that made Belleek famous, so they foolishly decided to stop producing Parian ware and revert to making ordinary household goods. This was a big mistake; it wasn't special so it didn't sell and the pottery became unprofitable. It was rescued by a group of local investors, who renamed it Belleek Pottery Works Company Ltd. They had more sense and decided to go for the top end of the market. They hired the artist and poet, Eugene Sheerin, who did a magnificent job. One of his paintings, called 'Innocence' (1879), showing a young mother with a child on a Belleek plate, is on display at the Victoria and Albert Museum.

Frederick Slater, a master craftsman, moved from England to Belleek in 1893 and by the 1920s the high-end porcelain side of the business was thriving once again. Since then the factory has had its ups and downs, especially during the world wars, when it concentrated on producing earthenware.

Fergus Cleary, the chief designer at Belleek Pottery, tells of Bill Thornhill, one of the men who once worked in the factory, who painted beautiful flowers on the pottery. Bill was very eccentric; he was also a likeable, affable man with a great pair of hands and he was excellent at his job.

Bill always wore an ancient, scruffy plus fours suit, the kind of thing that was fashionable during the 1930s, and he loved rats. He lived beside the graveyard and encouraged the rats living there to come and visit him. He fed them regularly, knew each one individually and could describe their differing personalities. The rats never did him any harm. They came into his house, sat beside him and enjoyed being petted. He gave the rats names of people who had been buried in the graveyard. If a new rat appeared it was called after the latest person to be interned. Fergus said the only rat names he could remember were Meeky Knox and Bald Rat.

I just love rats!

His neighbours became very worried when Bill decided he didn't want to live in a house. He dug a sort of hole for himself, put a piece of corrugated iron over it and lived in there along with his furry friends.

Bill was a decent man, who was very good to his neighbours. He did small jobs for them and they were very fond of him. They worried more and more about his welfare and the terrible conditions in which he lived, and wondered what they could do to help. They felt there was no point in arranging for him to live in a proper house again; he hadn't been content in the perfectly good one he once had. Eventually they decided the best thing they could do was to build a hut for him. They clubbed together and raised enough money to buy the necessary materials, bought a bed, a chair, a cooking stove, installed electricity and gave him an electric fire. Bill was given everything he needed. The only trouble was he didn't like it; he refused to move out of his hole in the ground. The neighbours wondered what they should do. They decided the best thing they could do was to wait until he wasn't looking and set fire to his old home. That did the trick. He moved into his hut and grew to love it.

Bill lived to be old and infirm. He spent his final years being well cared for in a local old people's home and he stopped talking to rats.

Belleek Pottery has changed hands many times and has expanded. It has an excellent shop, showroom and a café with friendly staff producing tasty local food. At present it employs more than 600 staff and has a turnover of around £30 million each year. There are interesting tours around the factory, during which participants are told about its history, have the opportunity to watch pottery being made and are able to chat to craft workers about their work. It has a nice friendly atmosphere, and you might catch a glimpse of the gentle ghost of unfortunate Robert Armstrong walking around the rooms he loved so well.

THE MARBLE ARCH GEOPARK

A geopark is a region of scientific value that encompasses geological heritage, folklore, local communities and educational purposes, which must be capable of sustainable development.

In 2008, Fermanagh's Geopark became the first in the world to cross borders. It stretches from County Fermanagh, in the United

Kingdom, into County Cavan, which is in the Republic of Ireland. It is managed jointly by Fermanagh and Omagh District Council and Cavan County Council, and it features on UNESCO's website.

The Fermanagh Geopark contains many places of historical and archeological interest, such as Castle Archdale, Marble Arch Caves, Big Dog Forest, Moneygashel Cashel, Gortmaconnell Viewpoint and Carrigan Forest. Prehistoric tombs, Iron Age forts and early Christian monasteries are scattered all over the landscape. It's the perfect place to enjoy a wide variety of activities, or to simply relax and enjoy the stunning landscape.

Marble Arch Caves

Marble Arch Caves are situated near Florencecourt village. They are named after a natural limestone arch, which is at the upstream end of Cladagh Glen. The Cladagh river flows underneath it.

The caves were officially discovered in 1895. Local people knew about them but they hadn't been properly explored. The caves are 94m deep, are more than 7 miles long and are a natural phenomenon formed by three streams draining off the northern slopes of Cladagh Glen. The streams join together underground to form the Cladagh river, which comes out of one of the largest karst resurgences in the United Kingdom. It is the largest in Ireland.

The caves themselves are spectacular and well worth a visit. They are full of glistening stalactites and stalagmites in stunning cave formations. It is a beautiful underworld of waterfalls, rivers and winding passages. I particularly enjoyed the relaxing boat ride and the 'Moses Walk', a dry walkway running literally through water, which is held back by walls that reach above waist level. The caves are very popular so it is advisable to book before visiting.

In the past the Marble Arch itself was used as a road by people who lived on Cuilcagh Mountain. There is a hole in the limestone through which it is possible to fall into the river below. One day a young girl ran down the mountain and over the arch. She was very excited and in a hurry because she was going to take her first communion. She forgot to look where she was going and fell through the hole. Fortunately her communion dress had a wide skirt. The wind caught it and it acted like a parachute so she drifted, unharmed down below. Some descendants of her family still live in the neighbourhood. They say it's lucky she took a shortcut to church, not to heaven!

Duffy's Circus used to visit Fermanagh every year and allow its tame elephant to drink from the Cladagh waters.

If you hear any tall tales about elephants living in Marble Arch Caves don't believe them. That story arose in 1912 when a group of German tourists were walking along the banks of the Cladagh river and saw an elephant go towards it and have a drink of water.

The Germans were puzzled; they couldn't see any sign of life, apart from the elephants and wondered if they were counted as part of Ireland's fauna. They went into a local pub and asked the barman if there were wild elephants in Ireland. The barman was a bit of a joker. He didn't mention the circus and said:

Yes! They can live here. The elephant you saw is part of a herd that lives in Marble Arch Caves. They used to belong to the local landlord until he fell upon hard times and had to move to England. He was an eccentric who owned a menagerie. He took his other animals with him but the elephants were too large to sail on a boat so he left them behind. They seem happy living in Fermanagh, but then who wouldn't be!

8

LANGUAGE AND NICKNAMES

Ireland, which is often described by its inhabitants as a 'wee small country', has produced four Laureates of English Literature: William Butler Yeats (1923), George Bernard Shaw (1925), Samuel Beckett (1969) and Seamus Heaney (1995). Samuel Beckett received his secondary education in Portora Royal School, Enniskillen, as did Oscar Wilde. The reason lies in the remoteness of the area combined with its past history.

The west of Ulster was the last place in Ireland to succumb during the Elizabethan wars. It was a wild region that proved difficult to subdue so Elizabeth I planted the region with people from the rest of the United Kingdom. These planters brought their tools and household possessions along with their language and that led, through time, to the development of Anglo–Irish.

Benedict Kiely once wrote: 'The most striking parallel between Anglo–Irish and Elizabethan English is the sheer delight in language for its own sake. The Elizabethan period was linguistically the most uninhibited in the history because it combined a maximum of art with a minimum of inhibition.'

Much of the Elizabethan English has been preserved in the west of Ulster in the form of sentence construction, vocabulary and grammar, for example the word 'yous' as the plural of 'you'.

The Irish are a talkative and adjectival people. They are in love with words and delight in vivid descriptions, malapropisms, double entendres, the lot! I strongly suspect that Fermanagh people love the latter most of all.

The region is remote. Many of the roads were little more than rough tracks until well after the Second World War. It's still easy to get lost in remote places! As a result much of the English spoken in Shakespeare's time, which arrived with the planters, has survived to the present day. Today many people in Fermanagh are bilingual, speaking both Irish and English.

The M1, which runs from Belfast to Dungannon, was opened in stages between 1962 and 1968. The road between Dungannon and Enniskillen has been improved and has transformed the lives of people living in the west of the province, but traces of the old language can still be found in Fermanagh, along with their local colourful powers of description.

Fermanagh people are, rightly, proud of their heritage. There are many local heritage organisations functioning to preserve it and they fought the good fight regarding preserving their townland names when, for the sake of simplicity, the Post Office insisted they were forgotten and BT numbers were introduced.

What follows is true throughout Ireland but is particularly true of County Fermanagh. The locals have a very expressive way with words. For instance, a stranger might say a man carried a wallet full of money. A Fermanagh man could say: 'Yer man had a wad of notes fit to choke an elephant!'

COMMON EXPRESSIONS

The following expressions are found throughout Ulster. They are emphasised to help people visiting the province for the first time.

'Dead on' means 'excellent, better than one hundred per cent' and not that you're about to be murdered! (Three less common expressions meaning 'excellent' are 'cracker', 'wheeker' and 'sticking out'.)

'How's about you?' often shortened to 'bout ye?' means 'how are you?' The answer to that is often: 'I'm dead on!'

THE IMPORTANCE OF BODY LANGUAGE AND TONE OF VOICE

It's very important to watch body language and listen to the tone of voice in which a comment is made. For instance, the word 'edjiot' means idiot and may be used as a term of abuse as in: 'Ye're a right edjiot, so ye are!' if somebody has done something stupid. Alternatively, if somebody has done something nice, such as saying 'thank you' by giving a bouquet of flowers, the recipient might say: 'Ye're a right edjiot, so ye are. Ye'd no need to do that!' That means 'that was very kind of you'.

CRAIC

Irish people love what they describe as a bit of craic (chat) so it's easy to begin a conversation with strangers. That often leads to hilarious exchanges.

If you want to talk to strangers everybody in Ireland talks about the weather so that's a good way to start.

TALKING ABOUT THE WEATHER

There are many ways of describing the weather.

Rain	It's a loverly day for ducks!
Light rain	A wee skiff; drizzle; it's spittin'; it's a soft day; it's mizzling.
Heavy rain	It's teeming; it's bucketing out of the heavens; it's comin' down stair rods; have ye ever seen rain the like?; it's lashin'; it ain't half coming down; it's pishin'; the ground's swimmin'.
A reasonable day	It's passing fair; it's middlin'.
A miserable grey day	It's a clatty aul day.

Bad weather	It's as rough as a badger's arse; it's a fierce bad day; it's a fierce dorty aul day.
Cold	Cowl, or cauld.
Very cold, freezing	It'ud freeze a fairy; it'ud founder ye; me pond's all froze over; the roads are like a bottle; it's quare an' cowl; there was a tight frost; thar's no hate; it's quare an' bitter; it'ud skin ye; it'd freeze the knickers off ye; it'd free the balls off a brass monkey (a brass monkey was the triangular stand on which ship's cannon balls were placed in the past. Very cold weather caused the cannon balls to contract so they fell through the stand); it's that cowl the animals are standin' with a hump on them.
Fog	(The word fog is confusing because it can mean a kind of delicate moss as well as fog) Ye couldnae see yer han' in front of yer face; yon's a real pea-souper.
Very hot	Awful dead heat; quare ball av weather; fierce day for the silage; the sun's splittin' the stones; it's quare an' close.

Yon's dead on!

WEE

Visitors find use of the word 'wee' difficult. A lot of subtle meaning is given by the tone in which the word 'wee' is uttered. It may be used in a variety of ways that are difficult for a stranger to understand, but then that's what this chapter is about. It may be used as a term endearment as in, 'She's a dear wee soul.' (She might be 6ft in height but she could still be described as 'a dear wee soul'.) The phrase: 'You're a poor wee soul,' could either be used as a term of endearment, or, if somebody's been complaining, it could mean 'catch yourself on'.

Wee may be used to convey a small size, as in: 'He's got a wee farm' or: 'Yon wee girl's wee for her age.'

Sometimes the word 'wee' is combined with small, as in: 'I'd like a wee small dram of whiskey' or: 'Look at that wee small lad.'

'Wee' may mean nice, as in: 'Would ye like a wee pint of the black stuff?' or: 'Would you like a wee cup of tea in yer hand?' ('In your hand' means: 'I'm not going to set the table but will give it to you wherever you're sitting.')

If you go into a restaurant and a waitress asks: 'Would you like a wee bite?' she's not suggesting she's related to Dracula, she's simply asking if you would like something to eat?

Sometimes 'wee' is used in strangely inappropriate ways. For instance, you might consider you had 'big hair' and go into a hairdresser to be asked: 'Do you want your wee hair done?' and be asked, when you're ready to leave: 'Would ye like a wee receipt?', meaning, 'I want to be paid.'

'Wee' could mean short, or alternatively, long, as in: 'I'm going for a wee walk.' That could mean only a few yards or miles. Similarly, 'I'll only be a wee while' could mean a few minutes, or a long time. I once overheard a man say: 'She said she'd only be a wee while but I could have soaped my ass and slid all the way til Enniskillen in the time she took.'

SO I DID, ETC.

A quirk often found is to emphasise a statement by making an appropriate repeat of a phrase prefixed by the word 'so', for example: 'I told him til wise up, so I did', 'They had quare craic, so they did', 'We were fed up, so we were', 'They are right pair, so they are!' and so on.

THOWL

Thowl is a simpler word for strangers to understand than 'wee'. It may be used either as a term of affection or of abuse, so again it's important to observe the speaker carefully and place the word in context. A rough translation of 'thowl' is 'old', as in: 'I'm away to see thowl aunts.'

Sometimes translation of what has been said needs careful thought, such as in: 'Lizzie was a great thowl girl. If she'd lived til Friday she'd have been dead a fortnight', and: 'If thowl Sammy'd lived he'd have been 100 tomorrow!' Auld Sammy could have been dead for years!

SEE ME

'See me' is another quirk of language that isn't heard as often as it used to be. It's used as follows: 'See me? See my man? See bacon? Can't stand it!'; 'See me? See my man? See cheese? Can't stand it!'; 'See me? See them flowers? Love them!'

ASKING DIRECTIONS

If you become lost the most sensible thing to do is ask somebody for directions. Fermanagh people are friendly and helpful. The only trouble is understanding what is being said.

When asked for directions nobody in Fermanagh, and this is also true to a lesser extent, throughout Ireland, is likely to say anything as unimaginative as: 'Take the next road on the right, travel for 2 miles and take the next road on the left.' You may be told: 'If I wanted to go to there I wouldn't start from here!' Then be given directions, such as:

Do you see yon big tree on the right, well ignore it. Jist drive past it and you'd find there's a wee small road on the left, so there is. Turn down there and travel until ye come til a crossroads. Ignore thon crossroads an' keep on going til ye cum til see a big brick bungalow. Drive past it and keep on going until ye come til a wee shap on yer right. Opposite it there's a T-junction. Go down yon road and ye'll come til a signpost ...

Sometimes locals, in their eagerness to help strangers understand instructions, will insert the word 'right'. 'Do ye see thon road on the left? Right? Turn left there. Right? Now go down thon road until ye come til a crossroads. Right? Turn right at the crossroads. Right? And it's the third wee house on yer left. Right?'

TALKING ABOUT HEALTH

Let's hope you remain healthy while in Fermanagh. If something goes wrong with you, or you know somebody who's ill, the following phases could prove useful.

Are you well?	Are you doing rightly?
Unable to sleep	T'was well intil the night before I fell over.
Been bitten by insects	Them midges ate the arms off me.
Bring up stomach wind	Belch.

Feeling tired	I'm knackered; I'm frazzled; I'm dead beat; I'm banjaxed; I put my feet up for five minutes an' fell over; I'm so tired I'm dead on my feet.
Not feeling well	I don't know if I'm coming or going; I'm all thuother; I'm run down; I'm middlin'; I'm up the chute (that could also mean 'I'm pregnant'); I feel as if I've one foot in the grave; I'm nothin' but an auld crock; I'm Donny; another clean shirt'll do me.
Feeling too hot	I'm not feeling so hot 'cos I'm far too warm!; the sweat's lashin' off me.

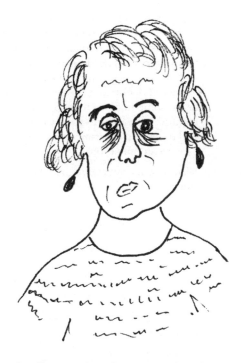

I'm not feeling so hot because I'm far too warm

Feeling cold	I'm foundered; I'm starvin' with the cauld; I'm cauld; me bones are caul'.
Tends to feel the cold	Cauldrife.
Stomach trouble	My stummick's turning; my insides are away with the band; I'm hangin' on the mantelpiece with my stummick; I had a gastrick flu that took the heels off me.
In pain	Wee bits av pains.
Vomiting	I boked; I threw rings roun' me; I wus talking til Ralph.
Depressed	I'm a bit down; I'm down in the mouth.
Feeling weak	I'm that wake I haven't a leg under me.
Very ill	I'm far through; I'm quare an' bad.
Long illness	I've been lying a long time; I'm lying with the dactar; I was quare an' bad; I was so bad in the hospital they sent for the big dactar (specialist); I was in intensive care and had tubes everywhere!; I had everything tuk out so I'm like a doughnut inside!; he was in danger of distinction. (Malapropisms are heard sometimes such as: 'She had a hysterical rectum', instead of hysterectomy, and: 'She had to have a sectarian operation', meaning Caesarean operation.)
Expected to die within hours	Waiting on; only waiting for the guid Lord to call me home.
Dying	Waiting for God.
Died	Got away; kicked the bucket; popped his/her clogs.
Itchy spots	Hives.
Feeling better	I could sit up and eat an egg; I'm coming til; I just stayed in bed until I got up; I'm far better.
Joint pain	I've a wee whinge in my knee; I've a wee touch av lumbago.
Sore back	Me back is broke.

Would you like to be buried with my folks?

Sore feet	My big toe's giving me gyp; I cud cry with my feet, so I could, they're that sore.
Sore head	My hed's splitting; I'm in bed with my hed. (You could 'be in bed' with any part of your anatomy that was being troublesome! The mind boggles!)
Pregnant	Up the bubble; up the chute.
Sexually transmitted disease	Clap, as in s/he caught the clap in Majorka (Majorca).

It's amazing how many people find romance while on holiday. If that happens understanding the following words and phrases could be useful, enabling you to know if you are being either deterred or encouraged. Just remember an old warning often heard in Fermanagh, 'Courtin' (pronounced kurtin') sends the head mad'!

STATEMENTS ABOUT WOMEN

A haveral	A big, brawny and awkward woman.
She's always scolding	She's a harpy; she's a wee targe.
Very attractive woman	She's a real wee doll; she's a wee cracker; she's wheeker; she's a humdinger; she's a wee cutie; see her – she's a wee wild bee.
Woman whose attractions are a bit too obvious	She's nothing but a big knock.
An older woman	She's not one of last year's chickens; she's no chicken; she'll no tear in the pluckin'; she's jist got a pullet's head.
Mistress	Fancy woman.
Wearing a lot of make-up	Has a right bit of slap on.
Has improved her appearance	Got her hur all done; got her face done.
Doesn't usually dress up	You'd hardly know her without the wellys an' the graip.

STATEMENTS ABOUT MEN

Older than he says he is	He's many nicks in his horn.
Old lad who's a rascal	Codger, as in he's nothin' but an auld codger.
Going bald	The storm's liftin' his thatch; he's rubbing his hair off against the bed-head.
Attractive man	He's jist a big hunk.
Strong, well built, big man	He's built like a brick shit house.
Womaniser	He's a bra-grabber.

He's a wee git

STATEMENTS THAT CAN APPLY TO MEN AND WOMEN

Wealthy	S/he lives in clover; has a power o'money; has plenty of doh.
Poor	S/he's stoney broke; down at heel; hasn't got what would jingle on a tombstone.
Looks great	S/he's cutting a quare dash.
Boasting	S/he's bummin' his/her load.
Too forward	Has a powerful cheek; has a right nerve.
Good lover	A quare court (pronounced kurt).
Always complaining	Makes a terrible poor mouth; always yappin'.
Difficult	Hard til stick.

HOW TO PROPOSE

There are two phrases that mean I want to marry you: 'I want til push your wheelbarrow,' and: 'Would ye like til be buried with my folks?'

QUARE AN' USEFUL WORDS WITH MORE THAN ONE MEANING

Blatter	Noise, as in 'yon drum makes a terrible blatter' or to hit as in 'she blattered head'.
Blu	Air movement, as in 'it blu a gale'; a primary colour, 'they painted the house blu'; sexy, 'he tauld a blu joke'; loud noise, 'the horn's blu'; swore, 'he hit his thumb an' turned the air blu'.
Bord	Bird, as in 'the bords sing in the trees'; get on, 'bord the bus'; plank, 'give us a bord til fix the floor'.
Brave	Good, as in 'he's a brave wee fella'; very, as in, 'them Cuilcagh mountains is brave high mountains'; courageous, 'he wus quare an' brave the way he faced her'.
Children	Weans; childer; caddies; coddies; cubs (boys); cutties (girls).
Clock	Timepiece, 'luk at the clock'; a wee black beastie with three pairs of legs, 'I hate them clocks'; hit, 'cum here til I clock ye one'; lazy, 'he just sits an' clocks all day'; hatch eggs, 'the hens are clocking'; go to the toilet, 'I'm away til clock'.
Close	Warm weather, as in 'it's quare an' close'; secretive, 'she's quare an' close'; near, 'she held him close'; those who share thoughts and feelings, 'they're very close'.
Cod	Joke, as in 'thon's a right cod'; joker, 'he's an auld cod'; lie, 'thon's a cod'; type of fish, 'wee Seamus sells great cod'.
Crack (craic)	Fun, conversation, as in 'the craic was mighty'; open slightly, 'the windy was opened a wee crack' ; not wise, 'his head's half cracked'; noise made by a gun or a whip, 'I heard the gun crack'.

Crater	A poor soul; whiskey or poiteen, as in 'I'm dyin' for a wee drop of the crater'.
Crock	Jar for holding water; container for fairy gold; somebody who is ill, as in 'I'm nothin' but an auld crock'.
Cut	Appearance, as in 'luk at the cut of her'; embarrassed, 'he wus cut til the bone'; not wise, 'yer head's cut'; injury caused by a sharp implement, 'Aggie near cut her finger off with yon sharp knife'.
Dead	Very, as in 'he's dead good at playin' his flute'; beyond help, 'she just dropped dead'; hopeless, 'it's a dead loss'.
Deep	Owes a lot of money, as in 'he's deep in debt'; or he's introspective, thoughtful, as in 'he's quare an' deep'; sulk, 'she's in the deep'; goes a long way down, 'he wus drowned in deep water'.
Durstep	A very thick sandwich, as in 'look at her getting stuck into you durstep'; plinth before the door, 'mind the durstep.'
Fierce	Very, as in 'it's a fierce bad day'; dangerous, 'yon's a quare fierce dog'.
Git	Nasty person, as in 'he's a right wee git'; get, 'git outta my road'; clothing, as in, 'you should have seen the git up av her'; rise, as in, 'Annie gits up at 6 o'clock' receive, as in, 'I git £60 pounds a week on the berrew' (Job Seekers Allowance, or any other type of national assistance).
Glar	Stare, as in 'she did nothing but glar at me'; thick mud, 'I got covered in glar'.
Gripe	Complain; drain.
Hoak	Dig, as in 'they're hoakin' spuds'; rummage as in 'I'm hoakin' in my drawers'.
Iron	Ireland, as in 'I live in Norn Iron' (local people often refer to the North of Ireland as 'Norn Iron'); 'like steel, his muscles wus like iron'; earnings, as in, 'she didn't iron much'; implement to remove wrinkles from clothing, 'she bought a new iron'.

Luk	Look, as in 'she luked under the bed'; good fortune, 'he's the luk of the devil'; somebody is looking for you, 'Richard yer lukkin'.
Naybor	No trouble, as in 'it's naybor'; someone who lives near you, 'meet my naybor'.
Norn	North, as in Norn Iron (see iron); none, 'he had norn left'.
Quare	Very, as in he's a very nice man, 'he's a quare nice fella'; queer, 'they're quare folk'. (Confusing because 'they're quare folk' could mean t'hey're very nice people'. It's necessary to listen to the tone of voice and observe body language to interpret this saying.)
Sax	Sacks, as in, 'put yer spuds in thon sax'; sex, 'he's sax mad'; sax, the number between five and seven; saxophone, 'he's a great man on the sax'.
Shuck	Shock, as in 'that shuck her'; a water-filled ditch, 'he jumped across he shuck'; the Irish Sea, 'he's movin'across the shuck'.
Skite	Go out with the intention of having a good time as in 'Big Aggie's awa' on the skite'; covered in drops of mud, 'I was covered in skites of mud'.
Snooker	A game played on a table with long sticks and poles, 'my wee Johnny loves playing snooker'; prevent, 'my big feet snooker me from wearing fashionable shoes'.
Stew	Traditional meal made from meat, carrots, onions and potatoes, 'me ma used til make a great stew'; 'it's your turn now, 'stew ny'.
Spittin'	Very angry, 'she was spittin' with rage'; similar to, 'she's the spittin' image of her ma'; expel the contents of the mouth, 'he kept spitting in the wash-hand basin'.
Thu	Put on, 'she thu on her coat'; finished, 'I'm all thu', (that could also mean 'I'm exhausted'); threw, 'she thu the ball'.
Tight	Mean, 'as tight as a duck's arse in a rainstorm'; drunk, 'Jamie wus as tight as a tick'; tight fit, 'this coat's too tight'.

Tuk	Go away, 'she tuk off'; remove; 'she tuk her shoes off'; stick in, 'tuk yer blouse intil yer skirt'; make smaller, 'his trousers wus too long so I tuk them up'.
Windy	A day in which there is a lot of wind, as in 'it's quare an windy'; window, as in 'my windy's broke'; suffering from flatulence, 'yon wee lad's quare an' windy'.
Whine	Complain, 'she's alwus whining'; an alcoholic beverage, 'she's right an' posh, she drinks whine'; high sound, 'the engine gave a wee whine, then conked out'.
Yer	You are, as in 'yer in for a right gunk!'; your, 'yer sister's a right wee cracker!'

USEFUL WORDS AND SAYINGS

Fermanagh people have great powers of description, so don't make the mistake of thinking there is only one way of saying the same thing. It's complicated, so complicated that I have suffered considerable difficulty in attempting to organise this section. The shortest word or phrase is on the left side of the page, along with those that belong to the colloquial dialect. They are in alphabetical order. The more 'wordy' translation, or translations, are on the right.

Word/phrase	Translation
a lot of	a clatter of; a go of; a lock of
a different religious persuasion	digs with the wrong foot; has eyes that are too close together; dances with the other foot
a drop of the crater	a sup of whiskey, or poiteen
a little of	a drop of; a bit of; a wee taste of
a mearin'	boundary fence
afeared	frightened

accushla	darling
aff	off
affront	embarrass, an insult
agin	against
alcoholic	a wild man (woman) for the sauce; nothin' but an auld druth; a terra for the drink; couldn't even stand up half the time; could drink a wild pile of stuff an' then plough a field
an easy life	the life of Riley
an unpleasant shock	a quare gunk
ball o'malt	glass of whiskey
barm	ferment
bohereen	stepping stones across a stream
boyo	man, or boy
bothy	little shelter house used when away from home
brae	hill
ceilidh	social gathering with performers such as storytellers, musicians, dancers, etc.
child	bairn; wean
citeog or cluty	left-handed
clever	there're no flies on … ; ye'll be the quare pup when ye grow a tail
colcannon	potatoes, usually mashed with milk and butter and mixed with something such as chopped scallions (spring onions), cabbage, onions, kale, etc. Traditionally served as a mound with a butter-filled dent on top along with a slice of bacon
conceited, self-important	he's up himself; ye shut hear him crow because he thinks he's the sun; he thinks the sun shines out of his arse; has too much ground under him

cor	a little hill
cro	pigsty
crockan	rough field
cross	crabby; crabbid; really riz; all riz up; lost her whole hair; with a hump on him/her/them; huffin'; go spare
damaged	banjaxed
ditch	could be a dug ditch, a hedge or a stone wall
dressed up	right up the oxyters (armpits); all wee dolled up
drouth	thirst, 'that big a drouth on me ah cud suck moisture off a cow's arse with a straw through a hedge'; thirsty, 'suffering a quare drouth'
excellent	dead on; cracker; stickin' out; the best thing since sliced bread
fiddling at doing something	futtering
finding life difficult	getting it tight
forbye	compared with
forrenst, beside	against us
forths	fairy forts around thorn trees
fulfilling the gesh	the curse or jinx comes true
ganger	foreman
gansey	jersey
great fun	quare craic; great value
griskins	pieces left over when a pig was slaughtered and cut into joints
guggering	planting potatoes
had too much to drink	airlocked; blocked; eight sheets til the wind; tight as a tick; drunk as a skunk
haggard	long barn
hauld	hold

hard-hearted	as cauld as a mother-in-law's tongue; hard as nails
hashin'	talking
hasn't much sense	ye haven' a titter av wit; ye have nae a gleed av sense; a little wanting; his/her arse is in a band-box; half cracked; daft; dulally; haven't the wit ye were born with; has a bit of a lack
he should be all right	he'll be grand if nothin' falls on him
I don't think much of …	no great shakes; no up til much
it's upsetting	it's diabolical; it's a terra; it's a blinkin' nuisance; it's a real torture
leavish	ugly
make a fool of yourself	make a right show of yourself
many, a lot of	a sight of, a clatter of, a lock of
march ditch	boundary ditch
maryah	my foot
mearned	bordered on
meathal	gathering of workers for harvest
messing around	actin' the cod; flaffin' about; actin' the maggot; doing it arseways
mummering or mumming	performing a mummers play
noggin	measure
not wise	edjiot; yer head's cut; in a daze; gaunch; headbin; if ye'd brains ye'd be dangerous; ye need til feel yer head; yer half a sandwich short of a picnic; ye haven't an ounce (of sense); ye ain't the full shillin'; ye've a wee want; yer as thick as champ; ye've a slate missing; ye shud be in the looney bin; are ye no right in the head; yer head's cracked; yer half cracked; hasn't enough sense til come outta the rain

ojus	terrible
overweight	broad as a barn beam; is beef til the ankles like a Mullingar heifer
pad	path
pike	conical haystacks
pishogue	wise woman, storyteller, can be thought of as being a witch
pissmires	biting flies, horse flies
porringer	container that could be used for either food or drink
quare	great, very
red	clear out, tidy
sallies	willows
scraw	sods of turf from the top of a bog
scut	brat
shaver	young boy
shebeen	drinking place, often illegal
sheugh	water-filled drain
sibling	planting potatoes
sinks	pits for refuse
skillet	similar to a frying pan, it's very heavy and used for frying food over an open fire
slipe	type of sledge, usually on runners, pulled by a donkey or a pony
stuck-up	wud have sardines for dinner and say they'd had fish; all fur coat and no knickers; has aspirations above their station; thinks his/her shit doesn't stink; has lace curtains on the windys and no sheets on the bed
surprised	boys a dear, thon bates all; s/he was so surprised she riz perches, so s/he did; it made my hur curl

talks a lot	could talk for Ireland; has a tongue that goes at ninety to the dozen; could talk the hind leg off a donkey
thin	see you, you're so thin ye'd drop down a gratin'; there's more meat on a butcher's pencil; yer fat as a match; not a pick on him
thon	that, same as yon
useless	as useful as an ashtray on a motorbike
very amused	laughed my leg off; thought is was the quare geg
very upset	tears trippin' her; crying flat out; cryin' morning noon an' night
whist	quiet; be quiet – hauld yer whist
yer	your, you are, as in yer daft
yon	that, same as thon
yous	plural of you (an example of preservation of Shakespearean English)

Will ye hauld yer whist!

COMMON, SELF-EXPLANATORY EXPRESSIONS

As rare as hen's teeth

As throughother as Maggie' Moores (Maggie Moore sold second-hand clothes)

Black as an ace of spades

Crazy as a lune

Crooked as a dog's (donkey's) hind leg

Could drive mice through a crossroads

Couldn't hit a cow on the ass with a bakeboard

Dull as dish water

Faster than greased lightnin'

He goes through toast like a cyclone

He's that suspicious he'd luk a gift horse in the mouh

High as a kite

Hoppin' mad

It'ud make yer glass eye water, it's that sad

It was like showing a red flag til a bull

Leppin' like a March hare

No bigger than a sparrow's fart

See you, if ye fell in manure ye'd come up smelling of roses

She died with all her fasillities (senses)

Small but beautifully marked

Soft as a baby's bottom

Them boyos is as wild as a mountain goat

They're so straight laced they'd never make love standing up in case they enjoyed it and began to dance

They're so unreasonable they'd not let ye luk outta yer eyes

Wet as a drowned rat

Wicked as a weasel

Ye put yer boots on in the morning an' don't know who'll take them off in the evenin'

She looked as if butter wouldn't melt in her mouth

Courtin' sends the head mad

EXPRESSIONS OF DISTRUST

Are you making fun of me?	Are you takin' a han' outta me?; are you takin' a rise outta me?
I don't believe you	I'll no swalley that one
Do you think I'm stupid?	Do ye think I came up the Bann in a bubble?
I don't believe you	Get away o' that; go on with ye
Are you attempting to cheat me?	Are you trying to take me in?

NICKNAMES

People who were given nicknames wore them with pride, looking upon them as a sign of affection shown by friends.

Some individuals have distinct ideas about how a nickname should be used. For example, Duck McConnell was a 'wee low fella' who liked his friends calling him Duck, but wouldn't allow children to do so.

Nicknames were often given to distinguish members of a large family, who frequently gave their children the same Christian name, for example Pat, Publican Cassidy and Pat Draper Cassidy and so on.

It's a bit more difficult to fathom the following nicknames – John Lunny was called Row, while James Lunny was called Todd.

Some families, such as the Maguires, are so large they have a host of nicknames, such as the Coachman Maguire, Jemmy the Coiner, Skin the Goats Maguire, Scotchies Maguire, Tommy the Soot, Maguire the Gardener (he was gardener on a great estate). His son was called Eddie the Gardener. Then there was James the Slates, Maguire of Doon, Maguire the Vehills, Lochy's Pat, Lofty's Pat, Blue Ned the Beggar-man Maguire, Paddy Puck, Goldy Maguire (she had golden hair), James the Staff and Johnny Snake.

I love the names given to the Curry family. The Whine Curry must have been always complaining (whining). Other nicknames were Bud Curry, Crafty Curry, the Bodkins Curry, Darky Curry, the Hanty Curry, the Kinats Curry and the Stand-up Currys.

Some people were given a nickname because of their occupation. For instance, Goose McDonagh was given his in the mid-1990s because he was what was known as a pack-man, that is a salesman who travelled around the countryside selling second-hand clothes. If somebody wanted something, let's say a suit, and didn't have the money to pay for it, Goose McDonagh was prepared to do a swap. He was often seen travelling around the countryside with a goose sticking its head out of his pack!

Haw-Haw was an ass dealer from Teemore. He skinned a dead donkey and left the head and tail on. He went to all the donkey fairs and advertised his animals by wearing his ass skin. The late Pat Cassidy told Vicki Herbert that Haw-Haw got his nickname because he gathered haws (red berries with a seed in the middle) from whitethorn and sloes from blackthorn and boiled them in his porridge, so his name had nothing to do with donkeys.

Percy the Millar was called Aul' White Face, Paddy the Bus was a bus driver, John Dolan, The Waxy Johnny Burke was a shoemaker and Mary the Tub, a washerwoman. Frank McCaffrey was called Barrowman; he wheeled a wheelbarrow and was an assistant to the weigh master in the markets. Some of the names of other market traders are Split the Diff, The Tangles, Johnny the Stick, Sam Brown, and the Big Milk Cow Man.

A smuggler from the Redhills area was called One of the Dodgers.

Some nicknames referred to an individual's characteristics, such as Roarin' Red Bessie who had red hair and a temper to match. John the Baron Brady and John Dolan, The Prince, sound as if they were 'up themselves' (see above). Big John Graham, Long Hughie, Big Joe Maguire and Long Fox were tall men, as was Big Francie Tummin, who was called Big Frankie. The Michael Teddy's were called Big Pat and Mrs Big Pat! Billy the Bird probably had one in a cage while Quiff Cassidy had a fine hair-do. Honest Arthur Irvine obviously had an honest reputation.

Other nicknames are intriguing because the reason for them appears to have been lost. Why was Hugh McBrien called The Officer? Had he once been an officer in either the army or the police? Why was there once a Johnny Look-up and an Ironjaw McKenna?

COMIC VERSE

There's a song tradition of writing comic verse evident throughout Ulster and very much in evidence in County Fermanagh.

I once worked in a school (not in Fermanagh) that had a principal the staff disliked. When staff were enraged by his actions somebody sent a child round, to each teacher, carrying a 'very important message' enclosed in a plain brown envelope. It had all the staff initials on the outside. When you received the 'important message' you read it, ticked your initials and tried to keep your face straight. It contained a typed, unsigned set of verses. They were relevant, hilarious, to the point and often risqué. The messenger would never say who had sent them. They had obviously been well warned. In retrospect, they clearly did carry very important messages; they kept the teaching staff sane!

Local historian Vicky Herbert, who lives in Lisnaskea and has done valuable work collecting folklore and knowledge about local history in old people's homes, shared a couple of parodies written by Bill Boles, who came from Enniskillen. The first one 'takes the mickey' out of Mrs Alexander, the wife of a cleric. She lived for some time in County Tyrone and wrote many well-known poems and hymns, including 'All Things Bright and Beautiful' and 'There is a Green Hill Far Away', and a typical Victorian melodramatic poem called 'Casabianca', which begins as follows:

Casabianca

> The boy stood on the burning deck
> Whence all but he had fled.
> The flame that lit the battle's wreck
> Shone round him o'er the dead.
>
> *Mrs Cecil Alexander*

> The boy stood on the burning deck,
> His feet all covered in blisters,
> He burnt his knickers up the back
> And had to borrow his sister's.
>
> *Bill Boles*

Bill Boles also 'improved' Thomas Gray's Elegy:

Elegy Written in a Country Churchyard

> The curfew tolls the knell of parting day,
> The lowing herd wind slowly o'er the lea,
> The plowman homeward plods his weary way,
> And leaves the world to darkness and to me.
>
> *Thomas Gray*

Bill's version reflects the down-to-earth approach of a Fermanagh man as follows:

> The day's done sounds the farmyard hooter,
> The lowing calf sinks slowly on his slat,
> The ploughman whizzes homeward on his scooter,
> And darkness falls o'er all, an' that is that!
>
> *Bill Boles*

BIBLIOGRAPHY

Chamber's Edinburgh Journal No. 308, Saturday, 23 December 1837.

Coulter, Michael D., *A Lakeland Heritage: Antiquities of Fermanagh*, Built Environment Northern Ireland Agency, 2013.

Edwards, Rodney, *Sure Why Would Ye Not?*, Blackstaff Press, 2015.

Herbert, Vicky, *Lisnaskea Workhouse*, Erne Heritage Tour Guide Production, Davog Press.

Herbert, Vicky, *Sights and Sounds of Fermanagh*, Erne Heritage Tour Guides, 2003.

Johnston, Jack, Ed., *Workhouses of the North West*, People's History (WEA), 1996.

Joyce, P.W., *English as We Speak it in Ireland*, London: Longmans, Green, & Co. Dublin: HM Gill & Son, Ltd, 1910.

Mallory, J.P. and McNeill, T.E., 'The Archaeology of Ulster from Colonization to Plantation', The Institute of Irish Studies, The Queen's University of Belfast, 1991.

McBride, Doreen, *When Hunger Stalked the North*, Adare Press, 1994.

Nelson, Charles, *Shamrock*, Boethius Press, 1991.

O'Dolan, Mairéad, *The Church Ruins and Stone Monuments Near the Holy Well*, Belcoo, private publication, Onedigital, 54 Hollingdean Road, Brighton BN2 4AA, 2006.

O'Muirithe, Diamaird, Ed., *The English Language in Ireland,* The Mercier Press, 1977.

Reihill, James John, *Friday's Child* (private publication).

Rogers, Mary, *Prospect of Erne*, Fermanagh Field Club, 1967.

Rogers, Mary, *Prospect of Fermanagh*, Watergate Press, Enniskillen, 1982.

Rogers, Mary, *Clogher Record Vol. 6 No. 3* (1968) pp. 606–617 (Clogher Historical Society).

Sheridan, George, *When Turkeys Chewed Tobacco, Memories from South-West Ulster*, Killesher Historical Society, 2001.

Yeats, W.B., *Irish Fairy and Folk Tales*, London: Walter Scott Ltd, 1893.